POLISHING THE APPLE 2

TEACHER DEVOTIONS FOR RESOLVING CONFLICTS AND
IMPROVING SCHOOL RELATIONSHIPS

DR. ELDERINE WYRICK

THE PRIDE

The Pride Press

Cedar Hill, Texas

Polishing the Apple 2 by Elderine Wyrick

Polishing the Apple 2

Copyright © 2018 by Elderine Wyrick,

The Pride Press, Cedar Hill, Texas using
Create Space Publications, Amazon.com

All scripture quotations, unless otherwise indicated, from THE HOLY BIBLE, NEW INTERNATIONAL VERSION®, NIV® Copyright © 1973, 1978, 1984, 2011 by Biblica, Inc.™ Used by permission. All rights reserved worldwide.

Scriptures marked KJV are from the King James or Authorized Version of the Bible.

The Pride logo and cover designed by Rik Wyrick, 2012, 2013, 2018.

The (Lion's) Pride Logo symbolizes dedication to the biblical principles of honoring God, country, and our fellowman. It reminds us that we are members of a family; we were bought with a price, and we are called to carry our cross of service to our "world."

More devotions by Dr. Wyrick can be found at

www.polishingtheapple.com, also at www.teacherdevotions.com

All rights reserved. No part of this work may be reproduced or transmitted in any form or by any means electronic or mechanical, including photocopying and recording, or by any information storage or retrieval system, except as may be expressly permitted by the 1976 Copyright Act or in writing from the author. The author grants permission to print/photocopy individual devotions for ministry purposes for no more than 20 devotions per year without written permission.

Wyrick, Elderine W.
    Polishing the Apple 2: Teacher devotions for resolving conflicts and improving school relationships. Cedar Hill, TX: Master's Pride Press, 2018.
    1. Teachers—Prayer and devotions. 2. Teachers—Conflict Resolution. 3 Teachers—Religious aspects—Christianity. I. Title

DEDICATION

I dedicate this book to my husband, Dean Wyrick. His godly example and spiritual leadership as a husband has greatly influenced my life. His unconditional love and acceptance have given me the courage to step out into the unknown and make my writings public. The patience and support he provided as I worked on the manuscript were remarkable. He is a gift from God to me.

TABLE OF CONTENTS

Dedication ....

TABLE OF CONTENTS i

INTRODUCTION vi

Overview of Book: vii

1   SEARCH MY HEART, O GOD 1

2   ESTEEM YOUR COWORKERS ABOVE YOURSELF 2

3   WALK IN GOD'S GRACE NOT IN YOUR OWN POWER 3

4   LET ME WALK IN UNCONDITIONAL LOVE 5

5   LOVE MY ENEMIES? 6

6   THE WORD OF GOD IS PROFITABLE 8

7   DID I REALLY SAY THAT? 10

8   ACCEPT COWORKERS UNCONDITIONALLY 11

9   CONTENTMENT IS LEARNED 13

10   FOOLISHNESS IS BOUND UP IN THE CHILD'S HEART 15

11   DO YOUR GRADES MEASURE LEARNING? 16

12   TAKE UP YOUR CROSS AND FOLLOW CHRIST 19

13   HELP ME TO BUILD A POSITIVE CLASSROOM 20

14   I DON'T GET ALONG WITH MY BOSS 21

15   APPLY YOUR HEART TO INSTRUCTION 23

16   STUDENTS WANT DISCIPLINE 24

17 AM I REBELLIOUS?	*26*
18 DO YOU LOVE ME?	*27*
19 GOD KNOWS THE HEART	*29*
20 HELP ME TO SOW SEEDS WORTH REAPING	*30*
21 HELP ME TO CLEAR OFFENSES WITH MY STUDENTS	*31*
22 I WILL WATCH MY WORDS AS I WATCH MY HEART	*32*
23 KEEP YOUR HEART WITH DILIGENCE	*34*
24 GOD, I THINK I AM ANGRY WITH YOU	*35*
25 LET MY ACTIONS BE FULL OF LOVE AND TRUTH	*37*
26 TEACH ME TO VALUE MY STUDENT AS I DISCIPLINE	*38*
27 YOU WILL HAVE ENEMIES; HOPEFULLY ONLY A FEW	*39*
28 DO NOT LET ME BE PUT TO SHAME	*41*
29 OUT OF CONTROL? BEGIN AGAIN	*43*
30 CONTEMPT FOR LEADERSHIP BRINGS DESTRUCTION	*44*
31 THERE IS POWER IN GOD'S PRESENCE	*46*
32 TEACH THEM TO BE WILLING	*48*
33 DISCIPLINE IS A TOUGH ISSUE	*49*
34 HOLD ON TO COURAGE AND HOPE	*52*
35 PRAYER IS YOUR LIFELINE	*54*
36 OBEDIENCE IS FOUNDATIONAL FOR TRUE WORSHIP	*55*
37 I NEED YOUR FORGIVENESS	*56*
38 PAIN CAN BE A BLESSING	*58*
39 WHAT GOES AROUND COMES AROUND!	*60*
40 FAVORITISM BRINGS TROUBLE	*62*

41 DO THEY HAVE A WILLING SPIRIT?	64
42 DON'T FORGET TO HAVE FUN!	65
43 I CHOOSE TO TRUST YOU IN THIS TRIAL	66
44 CALLED TO MAKE A DIFFERENCE	67
45 A SEASON AND A TIME FOR EVERYTHING	69
46 ARE YOUR JOKES FUNNY? ARE THEY HURTFUL?	71
47 IS YOUR SENSE OF DUTY TOO EXTREME?	72
48 WHAT DOES THE LORD REQUIRE OF ME?	73
49 OBEDIENCE IS BETTER THAN FORGIVENESS	75
50 GOD CAN BE TRUSTED IN THE STORM	77
51 TEACH US TO BE SLOW TO QUARREL	78
52 HUMILITY COMES BEFORE HONOR	79
53 GRANT ME A CHEERFUL HEART	80
54 BRING THE CHILDREN TO ME	81
55 YOU CAN CHANGE YOUR ATTITUDE	83
56 I NEED GOD'S WISDOM FOR THIS SITUATION	85
57 TWO ATTITUDES THAT SUSTAIN US THROUGH TRIALS	86
58 COMPASSION IS NOT CONVENIENT!	88
59 CHOICES HAVE CONSEQUENCES	90
60 DISCIPLINE REQUIRES ACTION, NOT JUST WORDS	91
61 LET PRAYER BE A NORMAL EXPERIENCE IN MY LIFE	92
62 YOU CAN BEGIN AGAIN	93
63 WASH AWAY THE "YUCK" OF THE DAY	95
64 TEACHERS CAN BE BULLIES TOO	96

65 WELCOME PARENT CONFERENCES 98
66 USE CURRENT EVENTS TO TEACH CHARACTER? 100
67 SUCCESSFUL LEADERS MUST BE MATURE 101
68 DOES YOUR GRADING PEN HAVE A HEART? 103
69 LET EVERY WORD BE ACCEPTABLE 104
70 THERE IS POWER IN GENTLENESS 106
71 PERSEVERANCE IS THE KEY TO SUCCESS 106
72 LEAD ME WITH YOUR VOICE 108
73 LOVE THE CHILD; CORRECT THE BEHAVIOR 109
74 WATCH OVER THE SEED THAT I PLANTED 110
75 BEAUTY OUT OF ASHES 111
76 HAVE WE LEARNED "AT ONCE" OBEDIENCE? 113
77 STINKING THINKING BRINGS DESTRUCTION 114
78 FORGIVE AND RESTORE YOUR STUDENTS 115
79 RENEW YOUR STRENGTH 116
80 OBEDIENCE BRINGS ILLUMINATION 117
81 ARE WE TEACHING STUDENTS TO BE KIND? 118
82 DON'T FORGET THE LITTLE THINGS 120
83 GIVE ME FRESH PERSPECTIVES 121
84 BE THE BEST TEACHER/EMPLOYEE YOU CAN BE 122
85 CHOOSE NOT TO BE OFFENDED 123
86 ALL STUDENTS CAN LEARN TO BE COURTEOUS 124
87 MY EVALUATION DID NOT GO AS EXPECTED 126
88 GOD HELP ME TO HONOR STUDENTS WHO STRUGGLE 128

89 GOD, I HAVE A DECISION TO MAKE 129

90 HELP ME LEARN FROM MY EXPERIENCES 130

DEVOTIONS FOR HOLIDAYS AND SPECIAL EVENTS 132

91 HOLIDAYS CAN CREATE STRESS 132

92 TIME TO REJOICE AND REFLECT ON GOOD THINGS 133

BONUS DEVOTIONS 135

93 DRIVE OUT THE SCORNER OR SAVE HIM? 135

94 GIVE US WISDOM WHEN SELECTING STUDENTS 137

95 CHILDREN ARE OUR MISSION FIELD 139

SUBJECT INDEX 141

INTRODUCTION

James 3:1 Not many of you should become teachers, my fellow believers because you know that we who teach will be judged more strictly.

My first year in the classroom was less than smooth. Below is a story that I wrote in Polishing the Apple, Volume 1. I wanted to include it in the second book for readers who missed it. The story explains why I value the many lessons I have learned during the past 30 years of teaching.

My Story:

With a red face and glaring eyes, she abruptly closed her book, pushed back the chair, stood up and declared, "I'm quitting! Any job would be better than this! I don't deserve this kind of treatment! Why would anybody put themselves through this kind of abuse?" And, as the startled students sat frozen in their seats, the first year teacher stomped out of the room to her principal's office where she promptly resigned.

I was that teacher over thirty years ago. I thought I was ready for the classroom, but I soon discovered a significant gap in my preparation. I had not learned how to handle conflict. But, because of a wise, experienced principal, I didn't quit. She sent me home to pray and think about my situation. I was back the very next day!

Returning to the classroom was like enrolling in "Interpersonal Relationships 101". As I learned to lean on the Spirit of God for instruction, life became my classroom, the Bible became my textbook, and experience became my practicum.

Teachers are expected to be role models both at home and at school. Educators shape the world of tomorrow. Teachers can cause students to "love" learning for the rest of their lives, or they can create memories of pain, rejection, and failure. Teachers can "block" the quest for learning by planting seeds of hopelessness and disdain for education and school.

Educators are judged by a different standard—even higher standards than those required by city, state, or government leaders. James 3:1 tells us that teachers will receive greater judgment. World-wide attention has been given to the need for quality, well-trained teachers. The world is crying out for higher academic standards. However, teaching academic subjects successfully is not enough. We must become persons of character who become examples for our students to follow.

Welcome to Polishing the Apple 2. I pray the book proves to be a useful resource for guidance, comfort, and motivation to be the best person and teacher you can be.

Overview of Book:

The Bible gives instructions for managing interpersonal conflicts and serves as the foundation for this book. The devotions were written for my staff and are instructional. Volume 1 concentrates on conflicts that commonly occur in a teacher's day. Volume 2 continues to address school relationships with an emphasis on the teacher's heart and attitude. Actions and reactions begin and are initiated from the condition of our hearts.

Teachers, administrators, staff or others who work with people can use these daily devotions for guidance in handling professional, academic and personal conflicts in a way that pleases God and builds Christian character in their lives. Communities will profit when these lessons are applied in schools, and nations will benefit as biblical truths are again seen and practiced in society.

Sometimes I fear that I am too direct and hard on my readers. I would like to write light and fluffy devotions that warm the heart. However, God encourages me to continually judge my own heart—to be responsible for the way I react to situations.

These lessons changed my life. By sharing what I learned through experience, I hope to help teachers through these same tough issues. Many times I failed the test and had to take the long way through to the promise land. A few times, I learned from my mistakes and made the journey without going around the mountain over and over again. Iron sharpens iron. My purpose for these devotions is to help you avoid those trips around the mountain.

A Subject Cross-Reference Index is included in the back of the book to assist readers in locating devotions that address specific topics.

Although this book addresses school issues, people from all walks of life can apply these nuggets of truth to any job or personal situation. I have found the classroom to be the perfect "model" for explaining "cause and effect" in relationships including marriage, family, church, and work-related conflicts. The school setting allows us to see the "under-developed, undisciplined" child in personal interactions. It encourages us to turn from our "selfish and childish" attitudes that create rifts and unforgiveness in our relationships. We can learn to accept personal responsibility by humbly submitting to the scriptures and the truths designed to give us the <u>true</u> experience of "life, liberty and the pursuit of happiness."

I pray that these devotions will prove profitable to you and help you to gain fresh perspectives in your everyday experiences both in and out of the classroom.

1 SEARCH MY HEART, O GOD

Psalm 139: 23 *Search me, O God, and know my heart: try me, and know my thoughts*

A major theme of this second book of devotions is "Search my heart, O Lord." Actions and reactions are initiated from the conditions of our hearts. If we allow anger, bitterness, jealousy, hatred, or unforgiveness to remain in our hearts, they will be reflected in our behavior toward others. If we fill our hearts with thoughts that are honorable, pure, loving, and forgiving, our reactions will be noticeably different. In Matthew 12:34 Jesus said, "... For the mouth speaks what the heart is full of."

Reactions are spontaneous. Too many say or do things that result in years of regret and pain. Words cannot be taken back once they have been uttered. The natural tendency of the flesh is to react with self-centered, self-serving, and unkind responses giving little thought to the long term consequences it may bring. As teachers who seek to bless and not curse, we must remain Holy Spirit controlled each day if we are to do what pleases God. The ability to give a gentle response during times of conflict develops as we mature in wisdom and self-control. Wisdom and restraint come from allowing God to reveal and remove unhealthy spiritual roots and attitudes.

Dear God, Once again I pray, "Search me; know my heart. See if there are wicked ways in me." If so, cleanse my heart from unhealthy spiritual attitudes. If there are things from my past that keep feeding wrong thoughts and attitudes, please lead me to freedom from the strongholds. I want to be like Jesus in all I do.

2 ESTEEM YOUR COWORKERS ABOVE YOURSELF

Philippians 2:3-4 *Let nothing be done through strife or vainglory; but in lowliness of mind let each esteem other better than themselves.* [4] *Look not every man on his own things, but every man also on the things of others.*

Setting up a classroom the first week of the year and closing down at the end of the year is a lot of work. Inevitably some teachers will zip right through the task and finish before other staff members. Each year one or two teachers struggle slowly through the myriad of required tasks while the rest of the teachers finish and were out the door. I observed this year after year over many years.

So what, you ask? I would like to suggest that offering to help the struggling teacher once you have completed your room might be a thoughtful and caring thing to do. Verse 4 above encourages us to not be selfish by watching out for just ourselves. The scripture above encourages us to be a servant to those in need. Sure, we want to get out the door and onto our own business, but God would have us serve our team members when we have the time and ability to help.

I worked with a wonderful group of teachers the last twenty years of my teaching career. I saw them truly form a team that supported each other. The goodwill and friendliness of the staff created a wonderful place to work.

I encourage you to be sensitive to the needs of your coworkers. When you have a chance, drop them a small note in their box letting them know that you appreciate their hard work. Offer to help when you see someone on your team struggling. This pleases the Lord. You may be blessed with lasting friendships from your team for years to come.

Dear God, Remind me to be sensitive to my team members. Help me to avoid being in competition with them. Show me how I can esteem them and be an encourager. I pray that you will blend our team together this year. Help us to learn to work well together. Help me to remember that you ordered my steps and brought me to this job. Help me to appreciate my team of teachers. I want to please you in all I do.

3 WALK IN GOD'S GRACE NOT IN YOUR OWN POWER

Romans 8:12-14 *Therefore, brothers, we have an obligation--but it is not to the sinful nature, to live according to it.* [13]*For if you live according to the sinful nature, you will die; but if by the Spirit you put to death the misdeeds of the body, you will live,* [14]*because those who are led by the Spirit of God are sons of God.*

In Luke 18:19 Jesus said, *Why do you call me good? ... No one is good—except God alone.* Jesus understood that the wealthy ruler was saying that Jesus, the man, is good. But Christ knew that no flesh could be good separated from God. In our natural state we are condemned because of sin. It was Jesus-God that was good—not Jesus, the man. The ruler was missing the full perspective of who he was addressing—not a man, but God in the flesh.

In John 3:6-7 Jesus said *Flesh gives birth to flesh, but the Spirit gives birth to spirit. [7] You should not be surprised at my saying, 'You must be born again'.* To have eternal life, we must experience two births. The first birth is outside of our control—the birth of the flesh. Our mother gave birth to our flesh, but God desires to provide us with spiritual birth. He draws us to his truth and to his love inviting us to be part of his kingdom, to be "born" of the Spirit by accepting him as our Savior to live in our spirit man. When the Spirit of God becomes a resident of our inner man, old things pass away; everything becomes new (2 Cor. 5:17).

Upon acceptance of Christ, the Holy Spirit lives within you, but because your flesh still lives, a war is declared between the Spirit of God and your flesh.

Roman 12:1 instructs you to present yourself as a living sacrifice—daily. Your flesh has a sinful, carnal nature and it will naturally follow a path of destruction. Therefore, you must crucify your fleshly nature daily and submit to the Spirit of God within you as you allow God to be your guide for today. Your carnal nature is "self-centered." The Spirit of God within you is "God-centered and others' centered."

If you are walking in your own power, your self-centered approach to life will bring strife. Walking in the Spirit leads you to trust, contentment, and rest. Are you striving today or resting? If you're struggling, choose to exchange your self-centered thoughts for God-centered thoughts of faith and trust.

Dear God, I admit that I am striving today. Forgive me for my determination that things have to go my way. Forgive me for questioning your goodness and taking matters into my own hands. Help me to relax and enter your rest as a choice. I give you control of those things that cause me to strive rather than to trust in you.
CR: Rest, Grace

4 LET ME WALK IN UNCONDITIONAL LOVE

Ephesians 5:1-2 *Be imitators of God, therefore, as dearly loved children ²and live a life of love, just as Christ loved us and gave himself up for us as a fragrant offering and sacrifice to God.*

The unconditional love of Christ is the most significant gift a teacher can give. Students will grow in confidence and security when we love them with the same unfailing love that Christ loves us. The gentleness of a teacher's soft answer and quiet tone creates a peaceful and caring atmosphere. Most students will respond well to love and kindness.

In times of misbehavior and required discipline, the love of Christ is your most significant tool. You must have consequences for the infraction, and you must follow the established rules. However, you can administer the discipline "for the student," not "against the student." To withhold consequences for misbehavior is to deny a student the security of the classroom boundaries. The student will test the limits; that's his job. Your job is to assure him those boundaries exist.

The specific consequence is not as important as the emotions you display. When correcting students, teachers need to be neutral; you are a tool of the law. The student is not coming against you, the person. He is rebelling against the rules of the school. Anger is not neutral. Some students have a need to test the boundaries. They will test the boundaries (rules) until they are convinced they are firm. Boundaries and structure in a classroom offer students a sense of security.

Should you become angry with a child, it is best to separate the child from you until you cool off. Don't discipline a student when you are angry. It is best to postpone the discipline until you can get control of your emotions. You may want to consider placing the student outside of the classroom or in a chair in the back of the room or some other safe place where you can continue with your work until your anger subsides. If you lose your composure or temper, the student will be considered the winner of the conflict. The student must never win! You are the adult. You are the tool that God will use to train the child.

Learn to forgive students quickly. Stay before God in prayer until you overcome any unforgiveness. Foolishness is bound up in the heart of a child--you are an adult. Your behavior should be above his. Force yourself to learn unconditional acceptance of the child by looking beyond his current response to what he can become after he is fully trained.

Dear God, Can you help me with my anger? I need help with the mocker that keeps tormenting me and disturbing my classroom. I want to be more like you. Teach me to be lovingly consistent like you.

5 LOVE MY ENEMIES?

Luke 6:32-33 *If you love those who love you, what credit is that to you? Even 'sinners' love those who love them. And if you do good to those who are good to you, what credit is that to you? Even 'sinners' do that.*

Learning to love the unlovely is one of the most valuable skills a teacher can acquire. No human naturally loves his or her enemy. In fact, it is only through God's grace and His unconditional love that we are capable of obeying Christ in this way. Jesus made this statement as a mandate for his followers.

How do we love our enemy? How do we love that disrespectful, challenging student that pushes our 'buttons' so often? Or the parent who always questions our motives and makes our job difficult for us? The answer, though somewhat simplistic, is profound. You can love the person and reject their actions. In other words, you can care about the person they can "potentially" become, and respect the intrinsic value God placed within them. You can love the sinner and hate the sin.

A way to test your heart for pure motive is to ask yourself, "Am I disciplining 'for' my student or 'against' them?" You can genuinely bless and not curse even an enemy if you can see them through the eyes of God. Allow God to use you as an instrument of His love toward your adversary. You will keep a humble, pliable heart and inner peace when you are willing to act out of love, rather than anger.

Does this mean that your adversary will change and never give you trouble again? No, unfortunately, it does not. We do not treat them with kindness to manipulate them. We treat them kindly because they are God's creation, and they have value. Their attitudes and actions are choices they must make. You only have control over your attitudes and actions. Determine to do good and not evil, no matter what they choose to do. You will grow in character when you decide to love and not hate.

Dear God, It is easier to say, "Love your enemies" than to do it. Fill my heart with love toward those that offend me. Give me your love and compassion for them. Allow me to have a servant's heart for each person that I meet today.
[CR: Love, Discipline, Conflict]

6 THE WORD OF GOD IS PROFITABLE

2 Timothy 3:16-17 All Scripture is God-breathed and is useful for teaching, rebuking, correcting and training in righteousness, ^{17}so that the man of God may be thoroughly equipped for every good work.

Without a higher power than man, all rules are opinions to be questioned, tested and negated. Without absolutes, man is left to his ideas as to what is right and wrong. The Secular Humanist philosophy has been taught in schools and the media for many years. Humanists want us to put away the biblical worldview and embrace a philosophy of "tolerance" believing that there are "no absolutes."

Here are some current beliefs prevalent in our society today:

1. What is right for you is not necessarily right for me.
2. Don't tell me what is right and what is wrong. I will decide for myself.
3. Man is basically good; leave him to himself, and he will find his truth and do what is right.
4. I am the center of my universe, and I will decide what is right and wrong. My standard begins and ends with me. No one can determine what's right for someone else.
5. Each person must be given a choice of lifestyle, and it is wrong to interfere with a person's choice by telling him he is wrong or by setting social standards of behavior. It is necessary for society to put away archaic beliefs of Christianity to have freedom.
6. Anyone who lives by "absolutes" and tries to put them on others is a narrow-minded bigot. (Some even believe those with absolute values are enemies of today's society.)

Moral standards affect every aspect of society. Caesar, the Roman Emperor, asked, "What is truth?" He asked this because Romans accepted many philosophies and gods. As society progressed toward "free thinking," sexual promiscuity and thirst for bloody entertainment, murder and mass killings became commonplace. History has shown that absolutes bring order and prosperity. A lack of moral standards and boundaries brings confusion, chaos, and destruction.

There must be a standard by which we measure truth. The Christian has that standard in *The Holy Bible.* The Word of God is powerful (profitable) for discipline. It doesn't just change our behavior; it changes the heart attitudes. Use it if your school allows it. Don't just tell students something is wrong. Let them read and interpret the Scripture verses for themselves. Use the dictionary to understand more difficult words. Ask them what they think it means. Help them to see that they are disobeying a holy and mighty God--not just you. Remind them that they will give an account for each action, and word. The fear of the Lord is the beginning of wisdom. We want wise students.

Teach the Ten Commandments. Students will not automatically know absolutes in today's society. Many churches are teaching good citizenship but don't realize they are failing to present these truths as God's law. Grace, taught by Jesus, completed the law; grace did not do away with the law. Law without grace leaves no hope. Law with grace explains what is wrong and then gives a way out of that wrong--a hope for change. Don't be afraid of absolutes. God's truth is the "Word of Life"1 John 1:1 (KJV)

Dear God, Help me to fill my mind and my heart with your Word so I can discern the truth from a lie. People everywhere are bombarded with secular humanistic lies. Cleanse my mind from these lies. Let me see the truth through your Word. Your Truth is absolute!

7 DID I REALLY SAY THAT?

Daniel 5:5 *Suddenly the fingers of a human hand appeared and wrote on the plaster of the wall, near the lampstand in the royal palace. The king watched the hand as it wrote. ⁶His face turned pale, and he was so frightened that his knees knocked together and his legs gave way.*

I faced my class with apparent dismay and began my rebuke with these words. "Class, I met with the principal, and she is upset because several of you continue to leave your coke cans on the bleachers. I can see 'the handwriting on the wall.' You're going to lose the privilege of going to the gym during lunch." I continued to lecture them about responsibility and privileges. I made it clear that when you abuse a privilege and are not responsible, you lose that privilege. I even reminded them of previous times when they were warned about leaving the gym clean. I finished by telling them how I was sorry for them, but there was nothing I could do. They would have to earn back the privilege themselves. When I stopped talking, one of the junior high boys raised his hand and asked, "What wall?"

I was confused. "What do you mean, what wall?" I answered.

"What wall was written on?" he replied. I chuckled. No one in the room had heard the cliché or the Bible story from which it originated. He had lost my entire message. As I talked about the mess in the gym, most of my students were trying to decide which wall was vandalized in the gym. It took a few more minutes of explanation before my message was understood.

Memories like these still make me laugh. It also reminds me how difficult communication can be. When addressing your class, you may want to check your message with them. They may not be receiving the same one you think you sent. You can do this "fast food style." You give your order at the fast food window, and they repeat your order back to you. You then correct any misunderstandings. In the classroom, you can check messages by asking someone to explain to the class what you just said, or ask a particular student if he understood what you meant; if so, would he tell it to you. Of course, you can always give a pop quiz—ha, ha.

Watch your clichés; they really can "date" you. If you use clichés, make sure they are understood.

Dear God, Working with kids can be fun. Teach me to be a clear communicator. Also, help me to develop that sense of humor that helps to break down walls and reach out to the kids.

8 ACCEPT COWORKERS UNCONDITIONALLY

1 Corinthians 13:4 *Love is patient, love is kind. It does not envy, it does not boast, it is not proud. ⁵It does not dishonor others, it is not self-seeking, it is not easily angered, it keeps no record of wrongs. ⁶Love does not delight in evil but rejoices with the truth. ⁷It always protects, always trusts, always hopes, always perseveres.*

We all have "quirks" in our personality. I have never met anyone that did not have significant strengths and significant weaknesses at the same time. So, how do we learn to accept the oddities or the unloveliness of each other? Paul gives us the key in the above Scriptures. Love is the key to your happiness this year.

The more honest I am about who I really am, not who I want people to believe that I am, the more I realize how human we all are.

- <u>Performers</u> seem to do everything right at the right time in the right way, and they notice when others are not measuring up. Their greatest downfall is judgment, anger, and pride. They lose a lot of joy in life because they either resentfully fix the things that others neglect, or reject people who don't seem to measure up.
- <u>Happy-go-lucky</u> people are always ready to play. They often neglect responsibilities in exchange for the now. They procrastinate on major and minor projects and create misery for those who depend on them. They tend to be self-centered, thoughtless, and self-indulgent.
- <u>Meticulous or perfectionistic people</u> must do things right. They worry a lot. In fact, they fret over everything. They can be overbearing in their expectations and slow in their performance. They are never satisfied with themselves or with others. They lean toward self-rejection, disapproval of others and preoccupation with things.
- <u>Know-it-all people</u> like to have a platform. They control conversations and seldom listen to others. They want to do things their way. They talk a lot but may not do a lot to help when needed. They tend to be controlling, manipulative and overbearing.

And, I could keep going. People's flaws are common. We all know them. But we need answers. And God has provided us one—only one is needed. LOVE the unlovely by appreciating their strengths and trusting God to help them with their weaknesses. The more I admit my flaws and commit them to God, the more I can accept other people's shortcomings. The truth is—we all need God. He created each of us with challenges that require His help to overcome them. Learn to see your coworker's flaws as God's tool for growth and maturity. God uses people to develop our character. I find that the things that irritate me about others are the flaws in my life that I hate. The more I let God change me, the more I can accept others. When I spend my time allowing God to perfect me, I am not so quick to worry about what God needs to do in other people. The more God changes me, the more I can have hope and faith that God can and does change situations as I commit it to prayer. When I choose to stop magnifying my co-worker's flaws and begin to concentrate on their potential, I am no longer their critic. Instead, I become their ally, a co-worker, and friend who wants to work and grow together as we serve God in our school. It allows me to love them without condition because I know that God loves me that way.

Love is the key. Love always protects (doesn't expose flaws), always trusts (believes the best until proven otherwise), always hopes (sees what others can become), and always perseveres (because God is not finished with any of us yet). Love builds unity among coworkers.

Dear God, Give me unconditional love for my coworkers. Help me to accept them where they are now as I realize that you're still working on all of us. Only you can change my heart of stone to a heart of flesh. I am willing to learn to love them with your help.

9 CONTENTMENT IS LEARNED

Philippians 4:11-13 *I am not saying this because I am in need, for I have learned to be content whatever the circumstances. [12]I know what it is to be in need, and I know what it is to have plenty. I have learned the secret of being content in any and every situation, whether well fed or hungry, whether living in plenty or in want.* [13]*I can do everything through him who gives me strength.*

Paul states that he has "learned to be content." He knew what it was like to be in the top echelon of society. Apostle Paul was an educated, "high class" citizen of his time. He also experienced being arrested, beaten, imprisoned, and rejected because of his faith in Jesus Christ. He knew the best of times and the worst of times. And, through it all, he gained contentment.

True contentment comes as we mature and realize there is a higher purpose for our lives than pleasure. Through life experiences, we often learn that the things we seek with our whole heart are still not enough to satisfy us. The young person who seeks popularity, a great career, a family, a home, a new car and nice things usually finds that they are not as gratifying as expected. This disappointment can lead to depression and hopelessness. Or, it can lead to a search for a higher purpose in life.

Paul discarded all of the "clout" as an elite member of society to follow Christ. It was in his commitment to Christ that he found contentment. Proverbs 19:23 says -- *The fear of the LORD leads to life: Then one rests content, untouched by trouble.*

It is not what you have or who you know that will bring real contentment to your life. But, instead, it is getting your relationship with God in its right place. Security begins with recognizing that Christ is your provider, your strength, your protection and your forgiveness. Allowing God to lead your daily decisions and knowing that God is in the middle of all of your experiences, good or bad, can bring rest and peace to your life. As you grow in your relationship with Christ and learn to lean only on Him, you will then become content no matter what your circumstances are for today.

As you acquire the spiritual contentment that comes from Christ, your students will be drawn to the "peace that passes understanding" seen in your daily walk. If you see them following you, when possible, point them past you to Christ. Help them to understand the difference Christ has made in your life.

Dear God, I am not always content. Sometimes I don't even understand what I am wanting. Teach me to find my contentment in you. Help me to realize that all good things come from you and you work all things together for my good.

10 FOOLISHNESS IS BOUND UP IN THE CHILD'S HEART

Proverbs 22:15 *Folly is bound up in the heart of a child, but the rod of discipline will drive it far from him.*

The tenth-grade boy raised his hand during study hall. I quietly walked to his study center and asked if I could help him. "The light bulb isn't working. Can I go get another one from the janitor?" he asked.

I hesitated for a moment and then told him that there was enough light in the room without the lamp directly over his study center. After I walked away, I saw him tighten the bulb and turn his light back on. He was playing games and trying to get out of class for a while. At first, this made me angry. I knew he would have bragged about tricking me if I had let him leave the classroom.

How do we keep from getting angry when kids play tricks on us? Well, the above Scripture helped me to get things into perspective. Foolishness is a natural part of being a child—especially some children. The reason we discipline them is to "drive it far from him." We should not allow ourselves to get angry over their foolishness; instead, we should see it as an opportunity to train and discipline it out of them.

This student's statement to the teacher was a lie. His game led him to sin. Children need to understand that foolishness often leads to wrong behavior. If they respect God's Word and desire to do right, they will hear biblical instruction and change their ways. This student earned a consequence for his deceit and lie. He was not disciplined for his foolishness.

By the way, a sense of humor helps to overcome your offense. Don't ever forget what it was like to be a kid. Much of the time kids don't think all the way through their foolishness. However, for some students, this response could be a form of mockery rather than foolishness. (Mockers seek to make the leader look foolish--Proverbs 9:8.) The same consequence would be appropriate whether it was foolishness or mockery. The teacher that controls anger or resentment during these times of irritation will be more effective in training up the child in the way he should go.

Dear God, Help me to be level-headed rather than hot-tempered when my students act foolishly. Help me to see these situations from your perspective. Their folly is an opportunity for training. Give me the grace to discipline rather than to react in anger.

11 DO YOUR GRADES MEASURE LEARNING?

Proverbs 11:1 *The LORD abhors dishonest scales, but accurate weights are his delight.*

God cares about your grade book. He cares about your test strategies. He also cares about your student's success or failure.

The marks you make in your book are measurements or percentages of learning. The degree of success that a student achieves is reflected in their scores. At least that's what most people assume and accept to be the case. However, in my experiences, it has not always been true.

I once worked with a teacher who gave a 20 point bonus on tests when students did "favors" like bringing him candy or doing special chores. Another teacher added test questions like "How do you spell relief?" "Rolaids" was the answer. "Relief" was considered wrong. I've seen other teachers take points off test scores because of misbehavior or failing to write their name on the paper. Are these accurate "weights" or measurements of education?

Grades are based on percentages. An 88 means the student completed 88% of the tested material correctly. How can we have an accurate measurement if that 88 is lowered by 10 points for failing to put the name on the paper, or 20 points added for special favors? And what about trick questions on a test? Even though they may be cute and enjoyable for the teacher, are they an accurate reflection of the material learned in your classroom? What about homework that was not done or an assignment left at home? Is the "0%" really a correct evaluation of their education? Or is it a measurement of behavior, attitude, or organizational skills?

I ask you to consider your guidelines for measuring grades. I encouraged you to be sure the scores in your record book reflect actual test scores and academic achievement. Also, it is more accurate for incomplete or forgotten homework, or papers not completed be dealth with in the discipline policy rather than in the grade book. Design consequences for these problem behaviors to encourage the student to learn new patterns and habits. When a student receives multiple zeros for no homework resulting in failing the course, what has he learned? This student hasn't gained much—at least not in self-discipline. Every test may have had a passing grade, and the student may have mastered the subject material, but his behavioral problem was never addressed. He doesn't need to repeat the subject matter another year; he needs to be held accountable for his assignments and be disciplined into correct behavior regarding his responsibility to do homework assignments. A zero is faster and easier to give than holding a student responsible. However, we are doing children a disservice by letting them take a zero rather than requiring them to complete the work?

I had a tenth-grade student who didn't turn in the assigned research paper. At first, he told me that he laid it on my desk, and I must have lost it. I called the parents to inquire about the paper and discovered that he had not been working on it at home. I encouraged the student to be honest. Finally, he admitted that he had not done the paper. I gave him an "I" for incomplete rather than a "0". I wanted him to learn to do a term paper. I met with him during lunch hours and after school to check on his work. The project was completed a few weeks later. This was his first report or long-term project he had ever completed. For years he had learned to take zeros without failing. He knew how to work the system and how to keep from failing. He completed his next project by the due date. The discomfort of having to meet with me those extra hours and knowing he would have to complete the paper, no matter what, was painful enough that he did not want to repeat the process. I did lower the project grade for being late by one letter grade but allowed the student a chance to get a "lower" passing grade if the project was done well. I felt the lost points reflected the need for re-teaching—thus a lack of achieved learning.

I encourage teachers to take this same approach with incomplete homework. Students need to complete the work and learn responsibility rather than be given a zero that destroys their academic average. The pain of being kept after school to finish homework assignments often encourages students to do the work on time in the future.

Dear God, Help me to give grades that reflect an accurate measurement of learning. Give me clarity of thought regarding your ways. Allow me to see each situation as you see it, and give me the wisdom to make correct judgments.

12 TAKE UP YOUR CROSS AND FOLLOW CHRIST

Matthew 16:24 *Then Jesus said to his disciples, "Whoever wants to be my disciple must deny themselves and take up their cross and follow me.*

I was 23 when I had my first child. I felt a little overwhelmed as they placed him in my arms and wheeled me out of the hospital to my car. I suddenly realized that this baby was my responsibility. I quickly learned the meaning of self-sacrifice. He didn't sleep much. He required a lot of attention and was reported as being the most demanding baby out of 72 babies in the hospital nursery. Quiet walks, hot baths, and time just for me were gone. My baby's very existence depended upon me denying my comforts to meet his needs. But I served him willingly because I cared deeply for him. He was God's gift to my husband and me.

When I entered the classroom, I was determined to be in charge. Things would be done the way I wanted them done. One of my coworkers, knowing that I was a new teacher, told me what worked best for her was to be flexible. She explained that unexpected things would happen, and flexibility would be the key to getting past the rough spots. My retort to her was, "Well, one thing I am <u>not</u> is flexible."

Guess what, she was right. Part of carrying my cross was to put aside my perfectionist attitude, my in charge approach, and my unbending schedule to serve the needs of my students. I gradually learned that it was not about me and my lesson plans as much as it was about the students and their success. I eventually realized that my students' success was my success and my students' failure was partly my failure. The more I owned the responsibility to see them succeed, the more I became willing to walk the extra mile with those that required it. God called me to help all of my students achieve, not just 80%.

I encourage you to discover what your personal cross is that God is asking you to bear. When you do, submit yourself to God, pick up your cross, and carry it with grace and love. Remember, when we cast our cares on Jesus, his burden will be light. You can find peace and contentment when you choose to accept your "personally assigned" cross. Remember, you never walk alone.

Dear God, Give me the courage to pick up my cross and follow you. Teach me flexibility and gentleness as I deal with all of my students.

13 HELP ME TO BUILD A POSITIVE CLASSROOM

Proverbs 29:2 *When the righteous thrive, the people rejoice; when the wicked rule, the people groan.*

The teacher determines the classroom climate. If your class is unhappy and full of strife, the first place you check for answers is in yourself. If you lead with wisdom, your students will rejoice that you are their teacher, but if you are unjust, moody, or fail to show the love of Christ daily, your students will not enjoy your class. Teachers should not be self-seeking or self-serving. Jesus laid down his life for his followers. He spent his time teaching, giving, healing, and serving humanity.

Without realizing it, teachers often create their own discipline problems through inconsistent discipline and a lack of routine in the classroom. Children follow better when the rules are clear, concise and consistently enforced. Mood swings confuse students. All of us have bad days, but, as professionals, we do not have the luxury of allowing our moods to rule our behavior. If you, the teacher, crack a joke and cause laughter in the classroom, do not punish the student who can't pull himself back together as fast as you would like. Instead, ask the student to get a drink or separate from the group long enough to pull himself/herself together. Teach your students the importance of learning when to play and when to get back to work.

Smile. Be personable. Be interesting. Have some excitement about your lesson. Be professional. All of these traits will help create a positive atmosphere. Students do not need you to be their second mom or big brother or best friend. What they want and need is a leader—a teacher who can connect new information to what they already know, to make the lesson relevant to their lives, and to offer a safe place to study and learn where they don't have to fear being bullied or embarrassed.

Dear God, Give me the grace to evaluate my leadership style and classroom behavior. Help me to see the truth about my shortcomings and my wrong attitudes. Give me the courage to change the areas that are out of order. May I always walk in submission to your will. Build consistency and a pleasant attitude in my daily walk.

14 I DON'T GET ALONG WITH MY BOSS

Hebrews 13:17 *Obey your leaders and submit to their authority. They keep watch over you as men who must give an account. Obey them so that their work will be a joy, not a burden, for that would be of no advantage to you.*
Romans 13:1 *Everyone must submit himself to the governing authorities, for there is no authority except that which God has established. God has established the authorities that exist.*

Dealing with an insensitive, unkind, overbearing boss can be tough. God sometimes allows us to be placed under a hard taskmaster to develop our character. That's tough to think about. But experience has taught me that God is more interested in my character than in my comfort. He knows that my most significant growing times are the hard times. And, He is willing to use whatever instrument is needed in my life to mold me into His image.

Luke 2:49-1 tells how the parents of Jesus, Mary and Joseph, did not understand why Jesus stayed behind in Jerusalem to teach at the Temple rather than head back home with the family. Jesus responded with obedience and became "subject to them" anyway. Verse 52 says "And Jesus increased in wisdom and stature, and in favor with God and men." His obedience to parents, who did not understand Him, pleased God.

You also can find the favor of the Lord by submitting to your leaders. As long as your school is not asking you to be immoral or break God's laws, you have a responsibility to follow their lead. If they are thoughtless and unkind, you can visit with them privately to appeal, but you must be careful not to gossip about them with others.

You only have control over your behavior and your attitude. Therefore, your primary concern is keeping yourself out of error. Pray for your leaders daily. Repent if you are rebellious. Humbly submit yourself to follow them, and daily deal with any resentment that may be trying to build. Cast your care at the feet of Christ. He has the "heart of the king in his hand," and he can turn it any way He chooses (Proverbs 21:1). Trust God. He has your best interest at heart. Rough edges are knocked off during the tough times.

Dear God, Change my heart. Fill my heart with love for my leader. Help me to follow without complaint or rebellion. You are the God of the universe, yet you submitted yourself to parents who could not understand you. Because of this, I choose to submit to my supervisor for your namesake.

15 APPLY YOUR HEART TO INSTRUCTION

Proverbs 18:21 *The tongue has the power of life and death... and those who love it will eat its fruit.*

WORDS: Words can be irritating, exasperating, discouraging, devastating, and meddling; or they can be encouraging, life-changing, discerning, supporting, and loving. Indeed, *death and life are in the power of the tongue.*

"Sticks and stones may break my bones, but words can never hurt me." This old saying is not true. If I hit you with a stick, it may hurt you for a few minutes or even a few days, but in a short time the wound will heal. You will be free from every trace of the injury. However, if I call you names, belittle you, or shame you with my words, the wound can live in your memory and heart for the remainder of your life.

Scriptures tell us that we will answer for every careless word we speak (Matthew 12:36). We are reminded that it is better for us to be thrown into the deep sea than to cause a child to sin (Mark 9:42). We cannot afford to lose our temper or harbor resentment or bitterness toward our students.

Keep short accounts with your students. Choose to clear offenses quickly. Pray for those who irritate you. Congenial students are easy to love, but a teacher must purposefully determine to love the challenging students. Allow the love of God to teach you how to love those students you find unlovely. God has promised that His grace is sufficient for you; he can take your lack of love and transform it into genuine love just by asking Him to do it. Do not live beneath God's promises. Let God's love permeate your heart for each student. Pray for unconditional love. God can and will miraculously answer your prayers. I know; I have personally experienced it. It works!

Why do we need genuine love for each student? Because I Corinthians 13:4-7 states *Love is patient, kind. ...It is not rude ...not self-seeking ...not easily angered ...It always protects, always trusts, always hopes, always perseveres.* These character traits will prepare teachers to lead their students to knowledge, self-acceptance, and determination to become all that they can be. Without love, the teacher is *nothing ...gain(s) nothing ...is like a resounding gong ...a clanging cymbal* (I Corinthians 13:1-3).

Dear God, Let blessing and not cursing come from my lips today. Remind me to ask for your supernatural love. Prick my heart with conviction if I mistreat my students. I want my heart to be a reflection of your heart toward each child. Only you can accomplish such a colossal miracle in me. I submit myself to your miracle-working power.

16 STUDENTS WANT DISCIPLINE

Proverbs 6:23 *For these commands are a lamp, this teaching is a light, and the corrections of discipline are the way to life*

You will have opportunities to practice discipline techniques this year. Students may try to make you lose your temper, or look foolish, or get you off track from your well-planned lessons. In spite of all of this, they are asking you to make them behave. In fact, they are hoping that you can control them and can teach them what they need to know. Students are insecure when the teacher is unable to control the class. When the teacher wins the confrontation, the students win too.

Make discipline your priority. You can't teach well until you have an orderly class. If you invest your time in training procedures and behavioral expectations during the first week or two of the new year, you will be able to teach more throughout the rest of the year.

Learn to "hear" and "see" what is happening in your class. Watch body language. It speaks louder than words. Watch for eye contact between the students. Listen for angry comments or irritation among the group. Don't allow "under the breath" remarks from one student to another. Don't allow rolling eyes, slamming books, or talking back. All of these undermine your authority and build resentment. Be willing to stop your teaching to deal with wrong attitudes—not just wrong actions.

Work to become consistent in your responses; students are secure with teachers who are predictable. Do everything "for" the students. They want you to be strong enough to control them. In fact, they are happier when you do. Go toward any apparent problems. Rather than worry about what someone might say or might do, be the first to confront the issue. This helps you to maintain confidence and control. If you think a student will carry a bad report about you when they speak to their parents, don't wait for the parent to call you. Be assertive and call the parents before the student gets home. Report the incident clearly and carefully to them. Also, inform your principal about the incident. This builds a fortress around you and allows the adults to work toward a positive solution. Do all of this with a professional, pleasant attitude. You will gain respect.

Dear God, Discipline is a difficult area for me. Give me a strategy. Give me wisdom and understanding about myself, my students, and your answers to my classroom. I trust you. I know you will answer as I cry out for your help.

17 AM I REBELLIOUS?

Titus 1:10, 15 [10] For there are many rebellious people, mere talkers and deceivers, especially those of the circumcision group. [15]To the pure, all things are pure, but to those who are corrupted and do not believe, nothing is pure…

"You are rebellious to your husband." I was shocked. Who me? I never considered myself rebellious. I never openly argued or talked back. How could I be rebellious? Then I heard it (in my thoughts) again. "You are not honoring your husband and allowing him to lead your family." I knew God was speaking to me through my thoughts.

"Yes, Father. Show me what to do. Help me to understand." I prayed. Then God began to deal with me regarding honor and submission—obedience from the heart. I knew it was time that I became more thoughtful regarding his opinions and needs. A few months later I heard my husband tell our friend that he had a new wife. He was not sure what happened, but he sure could tell the difference. Praise the Lord!

Passive rebellion—that is the correct term for my type of behavior. I never said no or talked back to my husband when he made a request of me, but I often ignored or forgot to do what he asked me to do. If I did not agree with him, rather than discussing my opinion and coming into agreement with him, I just ignored what he had to say and did it my way. I was not part of the team.

Do the above paragraphs make you angry? Are you thinking, "She shouldn't have to obey her husband if she doesn't agree with him"? Colossians 3:18 says, "Wives, submit to your husbands, as is fitting in the Lord." My husband's requests were neither harsh nor excessive. Looking back now, I realize that I was the one that was unreasonable.

Rebellion is rampant in today's society. It is so familiar that often we do not recognize it. Isaiah 58 warns us about the consequences of rebellion. People seek God and seem eager to know His ways, but they continue to do as they please, quarreling and fighting. They miss God's blessings and the Joy of the Lord because they choose their way rather than the way of obedience.

Obedience is the foundation of all character. Search your heart. Are you rebellious or obedient to your leaders? Remember, "...everyone who is fully trained will be like his teacher (Luke 6:40)." If you want respectful students, you must plant seeds of respect and obedience in your own life. Humble yourself before God and allow him to reveal hidden sin in your heart. You can become a new person too.

Dear God, I don't want to be rebellious. Change my heart, O God, and renew a right spirit in me (Ps. 51:10).

18 DO YOU LOVE ME?

Psalm 36:7 *How priceless is your unfailing love! Both high and low among men find refuge in the shadow of your wings.*

I met my husband when I was 12, and he was 14. Our unusual dating pattern began when I was 16. Dean called me once every month to ask me out for a Saturday night. I didn't hear from him again until 5:30 p.m. on the second Tuesday of each month when he asked me out for the third Saturday. After ten months of once-a-month dating, I realized how much I cared for him. In fact, I knew I was falling in love with him, but I wasn't sure how he felt about me.

In June, at the end of our monthly date, Dean asked me if he could call me about 2:00 a.m. during his midnight shift at the bakery. I agreed. I waited up until 3:30 a.m. and finally went to bed wondering why he didn't call.

The next morning my dad woke me up and told me that Dean had been in an accident. My heart stopped! "What kind of an accident? Is he okay?" I asked. My dad didn't know. He said that Dean was asking for me. Dean's mother called my house, but she didn't give any details. My imaginations ran wild. I dressed quickly, and my dad took me to the hospital. Dean had crushed his hand in a dough-rolling machine early in the shift.

He was in a lot of pain, but when I saw him, my heart leaped. I knew he loved me!

My discovery of God's love was also dramatic for me. Although I gave my life to Jesus when I was eight and made a lifetime commitment to follow him at twelve, I didn't honestly know that God loved me unconditionally until I was thirty. I will never forget the moment when the revelation of God's love dropped from my head to my heart. I cried. I rejoiced. I marveled. And, again, I committed my life to Christ, but this time out of love, not duty.

When you know that you are loved, you feel secure. You feel safe enough to be real; you find the freedom to discover who you really are. I "escaped like a bird out of the fowler's snare" Ps. 124:7 No more condemnation. I was loved, accepted and forgiven.

Do you know that Jesus loves you? Do you understand that He not only died for you but also continually watches over you (Ps. 121:7-8)? God begins the relationship with you by wooing you. He then continues to draw you to Himself to complete the good work in you that he starts (Job 36:16; Phil 1:6). God chose you and purchased you with his son's blood; you are not your own (John 15:16; 1 Cor. 6:20). He asks you not to strive but to follow, not to fret but to trust, not to change yourself but to allow God to do the work in you. He is all-sufficient; find your refuge in his sufficiency not your own. Jesus loves you!

Dear God, Thank you for your unfailing love. Open my eyes and help me to see the truth. I want to love you more.

19 GOD KNOWS THE HEART

Psalm 44:21 *Would not God have discovered it, since he knows the secrets of the heart?*

I couldn't believe the boy jumped on her back. He was a tall eighth grader, and she was a petite seventh grader. John had never been aggressive before. He was sometimes careless and rowdy, but not mean. Questions still filled my thoughts as John's parents, his teachers and I took our seats in the conference room. After prayer, the principal asked the teacher to give her report. The teacher reported that John and the young lady were on the playground with the other students when John came up from behind and jumped on her back—piggyback style. The startled girl fell to the ground and began to cry. The teacher came to her assistance, and John was taken to the office.

John seemed somewhat frustrated, embarrassed and a little confused as the teacher gave the report. The more we asked him "why?", the more difficulty he had explaining himself. No, he wasn't trying to hurt her. No, he wasn't mad at her. No, he wasn't trying to show off to the other guys. He was just playing. Finally, the truth came out. He liked her. He was flirting with her.

John hadn't matured enough to realize that guys jump on other guys' backs, but girls don't like that. He discovered that girls cry when you jump on them. With some fatherly counsel, a small consequence and an apology to the girl, the issue was settled.

Educators must not be too hasty to assume we understand the motive of the actions. Two different students can do the same action for entirely different reasons. Asking questions and allowing the student to explain and confess is the best approach. Also, be willing to look at issues through a child's eyes. Then, you will be able to help the student understand the issue from an adult's perspective. Unless the student understands the problem, he/she will feel you are overbearing and unfair.

Dear God, Give me ears to hear my student's heart. Help me to discover the root causes of misbehavior. Continue to teach me sensitivity and wisdom as I deal with unexpected discipline issues.

20 HELP ME TO SOW SEEDS WORTH REAPING

Job 4:8 *As I have observed, those who plow evil and those who sow trouble reap it.*
James 3:17-18 *Peacemakers who sow in peace raise a harvest of righteousness.*

Teachers, as well as students, want to be treated properly. They want to be accepted, to feel loved, and to know that their opinion is heard. Unfortunately, too many don't realize that honor and respect are earned. They are not automatic rights.

A student brings an unusual report to the teacher. What will cause her to listen? A teacher has a creative idea or another way to do something. What will make the administrator interested? An irate parent brings a negative report about a teacher to the principal. What will cause the principal to stand up for the teacher? The answer to all three of these questions is the same. The person's reputation and his past behavior affect the authority's response. These are times of reaping what you sowed.

Proverbs tells us that those who are faithful and loving will find favor and have a good reputation in the sight of God and man (Proverbs 3:3-4). Obedient students earn privileges and trust. Responsible teachers earn respect, renewed contracts, and positive relationships with students, parents, and the principal. Godly leaders bring blessing and peace to a school (Proverbs 29:2). Each of these examples shows the principle of sowing good seed and then reaping blessings. *Do not be deceived: God cannot be mocked. A man reaps what he sows* (Galatians 6:7).

Each day examine your seeds. Are your actions righteous? Will they bring good fruit to you later? Are you blessing or cursing others? Are you supporting leadership or criticizing them? Are you completely obeying your directives? Are you diligent in your responsibilities? Are you showing yourself to be trustworthy? If not, you can change your sowing today. Plant good seeds today, and after many days you will reap a good harvest.

Dear God, Examine my heart to see if unrighteous seeds are being sown. Forgive me where I have failed. Forgive me for my stubbornness and my self-will. With your help, I will choose to plant good seeds today.

21 HELP ME TO CLEAR OFFENSES WITH MY STUDENTS

Proverbs 18:19 *An offended brother is more unyielding than a fortified city, and disputes are like the barred gates of a citadel.*

As a Christian teacher, my greatest desire is to walk as Jesus walked so I can lead others to the foot of the cross. The above verse reminds me that an offended student will not only refuse to follow me to the cross but will build "bars" around his heart and not allow any of God's truth that I teach penetrate his mind. If I offend a student, I have become a stumbling block to his walk with Christ.

"I did what was right! He asked for it, and I gave it to him!" I reasoned with myself. But the truth remained; I had offended a little one. Jesus said in Luke 17:2 that it would be better that a millstone be hung around my neck, and I be thrown into the deepest sea than to offend a little one. Ou-Ou-Ouch! That's hard. I am held responsible because I am the adult.

"Well, okay. How do I correct it?" I asked. Matthew 5:23-24 instructs me to leave my gift at the altar and make it right with my fellowman and then return to the altar. I must apologize. My apology is not for the "correction" that I gave, but for the lack of love and the wrong attitude that I used when I corrected my student. All correction must be "for" my students, not against them. The correction process is not complete until I restore my student back to the classroom and to me as a person. This is the only way to avoid "walls" of communication. A student who is cut off from communication is a student who cannot and will not be taught.

Dear God, Forgive me for offending my students. Forgive me for taking their behavior personally. Teach me to restore as I discipline; give me wisdom today to break the emotional walls down between us.

22 I WILL WATCH MY WORDS AS I WATCH MY HEART

Romans 3:13-14 *Their throats are open graves; their tongues practice deceit. The poison of vipers is on their lips." ¹⁴ "Their mouths are full of cursing and bitterness.*

According to Luke 6:45, the words we say reflect the spiritual condition of our hearts. More and more I understand that my attitudes shape my thoughts and my words. When I stuff anger and hurt and then refuse to work through conflicts, my words become bitter and attacking. Disagreements and anger that are allowed to linger affect how I perceive my world. It's like looking through a colored lens that changes the color of everything around me.

Today's Scripture refers to the throat as a tunnel from the heart to the tongue. It is an open "grave"—a place of death for those whose hearts are continually evil. The words of these transgressors are poison to everyone; they are full of deception, cursing, bitterness, and death. Their antagonism reflects a heart that is out of fellowship with God—a heart that has allowed darkness to overshadow good.

I prefer to think this verse refers only to non-believers; however, all of us fall short of God's best (Romans 3:10). 1 John

1:8 tells us that there is no one without sin. And, my experience convinces me that I can build bitterness and anger in my heart even though I am a child of God. If I allow darkness to shadow my heart, it will tinge my outlook on life. And, my mouth will reveal my heart's condition through unkind, thoughtless words.

Bitter and angry words warn me of the need to make my heart right with God and my fellowman. I must put on humility and submit myself before God's throne. I then allow Him to cleanse my heart so that my words become pure. With God's unlimited power, with His mercy and His grace, He changes my heart and renews my mind because of my repentance.

As we daily walk upright before God, taking the log out of our own eye, we will be able to help our students get their splinters out too (Matthew 7:3-5). In other words, teachers who continually cleanse their hearts before the Lord will be better prepared to help their students see their need for restoration with their friends, parents, and teachers.

Dear God, Help me to quickly recognize the times when my heart begins to fill with bitterness and anger. I want to commit myself to keeping short accounts with my fellowman and with you. Let my words be pure and pleasant as you purify my heart once again.

23 KEEP YOUR HEART WITH DILIGENCE

Proverbs 4:23 *Keep thy heart with all diligence; for out of it are the issues of life.* (KJV)

Attitudes make or break our day. One look or one wrong word can destroy a good day. What happened? What caused the dramatic change? Perhaps, without our knowledge, we have developed a "heart" problem. Unresolved issues with our family, neighbor, coworker or with God Himself can cause this malfunction of the spiritual "heart." Unsettled issues create rifts or divisions in our lives that affect the attitudes of our hearts.

Scripture tells us to watch over our heart because it affects our entire day. How do we "keep our heart with all diligence"? In Jeremiah 17:9 we read, *The heart is deceitful above all things and beyond cure. Who can understand it?* I believe that only the Holy Spirit can reveal our real motives and the condition of our heart! David prayed, *Create in me a clean heart, O God, and renew a right spirit within me.* (Psalm 51:10) He realized that only God could set his heart and attitude right again.

As I become aware of my heart issues, I cry out to God for help. I first confess with my mouth that things are not right (even when I don't know the root issues). Then, I ask God to reveal to me where I have wronged my fellowman and to show me how to make things right. Next, I spend time reading a related passage of Scripture--meditating on it--looking for truth to apply to my situation. Finally, when the Holy Spirit reveals the truth to me and brings conviction, I repent and commit myself to do what is required to clear the offense.

I know that the Holy Spirit can set your heart right again. He has done it for me time and again. Your peace and joy depend upon a clean heart. A pure heart comes when you take care of offenses. Be assured that *He who began a good work in you, will carry it on to completion...* (Phil.1:6). He's just a prayer away!

Dear God, Please do heart surgery on me. Take my heart of stone and replace it with a heart of flesh (Ezek. 11:19) *Let the words of my mouth and the meditations of my heart be acceptable in Thy sight, O Lord, my Strength and my Redeemer* (Psalm 19:14). Without your help, I can't change my heart.

24 GOD, I THINK I AM ANGRY WITH YOU

Psalm 71:20-21 *Though you have made me see troubles, many and bitter, you will restore my life again; from the depths of the earth you will again bring me up.*[21] *You will increase my honor and comfort me once more.*

Admitting you are angry with God is the first step to finding the answer to your unresolved situation. Sometimes we pray, and no response comes—at least no answer that we can understand or see. Whether we are facing the loss of a loved one, an unexpected illness, a financial crisis, the betrayal of a friend, the loss of a dream, or another personal issue, our thoughts often accuse God of being unloving, unkind, and non-caring. Knowing that God has the power to stop the pain and right the wrong but doesn't do anything to bring relief, is a test of our faith. Is God directing our path? Does he really have every hair on our head numbered? Does He understand our trials and pain? If so, why is He taking me through this valley? Why is He so silent? Why me?

I admit that I have had several times in my life where I couldn't put the puzzle pieces together to understand "why?" How could God allow this tragedy or injustice? It was the loss of my father that caused me to question. I prayed for his healing and waited expectantly for the miracle that never came. I was faced with choosing how I would respond to the unanswered prayers. Thoughts of anger, unfairness, confusion, and sadness bombarded my mind. As I struggled before God with these feelings, I remembered a hymn I often heard in my church as a child—"Needing a friend to help me in the end, Where could I go, but to the Lord." The truth of this hymn sank deep into my thoughts. It was true; there was nowhere else to go but to God.

God is my foundation. It was then I made a conscious decision to submit to God and trust Him. I submitted to God's sovereignty and His plan. I began to realize that His purposes are greater than my ability to comprehend. In essence, I chose to "forgive God," to release my anger, lay down my unanswered questions, take up my cross and follow Christ. As soon as I released my anger, I felt peace. I experienced the truth of what Jesus said in Matthew 11:28 "Come to me, all you who are weary and burdened, and I will give you rest." In this lifetime, I will probably never understand why, but I learned a valuable lesson about letting God be God. Trust and obey are the two foundational truths that helped me through difficult times. I chose to let God be God.

Signs of anger toward God include a lack of church attendance, inability to pray, avoiding the Bible, generalized anger and bitterness, and a loss of genuine feelings of love for others. Each of these responses influences your performance as a teacher. In my struggle, I realized that God was there all the time, watching, waiting and caring for me. My response was to repent for judging God, submit to his sovereignty and choose to believe Romans 8:28 "And we know that in all things God works for the good of those who love him, who[a] have been called according to his purpose."

Dear God, Minister to those who are angry, hurting, and disillusioned. Pour your love out to them and bring comfort to their grief and pain. Bring sunshine where there is rain, and bring hope where there is hopelessness. Teach us to choose to trust you more. You are sovereign.

25 LET MY ACTIONS BE FULL OF LOVE AND TRUTH

I John 3:18 *Dear children, let us not love with words or tongue but with actions and in truth.*

Students will remember who you are more than what you teach. They will recognize insincerity and double standards in a leader's life. As we instruct our students to love each other and to accept differences, we must guard ourselves to be sure that we are consistently living what we teach. Unconditional love draws out the best in others. Love reflects our Savior. Love brings people to the foot of the cross. Love brings change.

Even though we may understand the above statements, often our daily lives do not reflect these truths. It is so easy to become philosophical and removed from the students (especially junior high and high school students). People often label students as rebels, losers, lazy, dishonest, immoral, and hopeless. As teachers, we would never write these labels down or even acknowledge them in a group meeting; nevertheless, our opinions become set toward individual students, and our attitude becomes evident in our reactions toward them. Unfortunately, many students are branded with a label and are never able to overcome its stigma. We, as loving, Christ-like, teachers can help a student find a new path and a fresh start through our unconditional love and our unfailing belief in God's ability to change people. We cannot force a child to want to change, but we can lift that child in prayer daily, love him unconditionally, and be there for him when he's looking for answers. We must never, never give up on his future.

Today, inspect your attitudes toward your students. Perhaps God placed specific students in your path so you could practice God's unconditional love. Instead of rejecting or just tolerating students with problems, ask God to help you love them to a higher plane--to a better way--to the cross of Christ.

Dear God, Teach me unconditional love toward my students. Correct me when I label and reject students that are difficult. Convict me when I am unloving. Teach me to reflect you through these challenging experiences.

26 TEACH ME TO VALUE MY STUDENT AS I DISCIPLINE

Proverbs 3:11-12 *My son, do not despise the LORD's discipline and do not resent his rebuke, ^{12} because the LORD disciplines those he loves, as a father the son he delights in.*

Solomon gives us the key to loving correction. Psalm 139:16 tells us that "All the days ordained for me were written in your book before one of them came to be." Our Heavenly Father knows the potential we have built into our being. He knows what we can be, and He lovingly and unceasingly leads us toward that path that we should go. But, when we rebel and choose an alternate route, He corrects us. Not because He hates us, but because He knows what we will miss if we get off track.

Teachers can also look beyond the present to see the potential that God has placed into each child. If you truly love the child, you will gently but firmly insist on specific behavioral changes when a student is acting out. And through all of this, you should keep your eyes on his future, not his present. Students are not always loveable in the present situation. Because of this, we must be able to see past the current behavior to truly love him through correction into a better path.

God offers you the grace to love the unlovely child. He said, "My grace is sufficient for you, . . ." Cor. 12:9) "If any of you lacks wisdom, he should ask God,..." (James 1:5)   Allow God to do the work in your heart—a work of unconditional love. It is a work of the Holy Spirit, not just a decision. Pray for your attitudes. Pray for wisdom and supernatural love for that problematic student. Pray for wisdom to understand how to approach the child in a way that the student can receive correction and eventually be grateful for your instruction. Remain in the presence of God long enough to be filled with His love for the difficult student.

Dear God, It's hard to love those kids that give me trouble. I want to love the way you love. I want to walk in unconditional love, but it will have to be your Holy Spirit that does that in me. I submit myself to you. Work in me what I cannot do in myself.

27 YOU WILL HAVE ENEMIES; HOPEFULLY ONLY A FEW

1 Samuel 18:8-9; 28-29 *Saul was furious; this refrain galled him. 'They have credited David with tens of thousands,' he thought, 'but me with only thousands. What more can he get but the kingdom?' ⁹And from that time on Saul kept a jealous eye on David. . . ²⁸When Saul realized that the LORD was with David and that his daughter Michal loved David, ²⁹Saul became still more afraid of him, and he remained his enemy the rest of his days.*

I was naive enough to believe that I could make everyone happy if I tried hard enough. I tried to be all things to all people. I took the blame for almost every conflict in my life and was determined to change to make things better. Consequently, I became a chameleon, but I still had enemies. Then the "light" came, and I understood that it was not sinful to have enemies. I had the responsibility to forgive those who offended me and to seek forgiveness from those I hurt. Nevertheless, I could not make the other person forgive me. I can keep my heart from bitterness and hatred by forgiving others even when they do not seek it, but others have to decide to forgive.

Anytime a person steps out to do something for God, to go against the norm, or to stand for unpopular convictions, in spite of peer pressure, they take a chance of making someone mad. Many people hated Jesus. Even the most devout religious leaders misunderstood him and rejected him. Jesus chose to keep going forward with his mission despite the conflicts. He did not purposely offend them, but neither did he consider himself a failure because they misunderstood him.

I think the only answer to conflict is to search your heart to see if there is insensitivity, sin or wrong motive on your part in the situation. If there is, you need to confess your error and ask for forgiveness. We must try to live at peace with all men, but even the scriptures indicate that it is not always possible (Romans 12:18).

So, what do we do after we've done all we can do, and they still reject us? We are instructed to bless them; we are to pray for them; and we can do good to them (Luke 6:28). We should never stop trying to be kind and loving toward them. Simultaneously, we must continue with our ministry by laying the situation at the feet of Christ knowing that he suffered rejection too.

Saul hated David because he was successful; he intimidated Saul. What was David's error? There was no error, but Saul continued to try to kill David. What did David do? He dodged the spears--and he continued to honor Saul as his king. He would not speak against him or do anything to bring him harm. That is the picture of blessing and not cursing in spite of attack.

Dear God, I don't like to have enemies, but I do. Search my heart for any unforgiveness. I choose to go forward with your purposes in my life as I bless those who have not found the grace to forgive me. Give me greater wisdom for dealing with conflicts.

28 DO NOT LET ME BE PUT TO SHAME

Psalm 25:2-3 ...Do not let me be put to shame, nor let my enemies triumph over me. ³No one whose hope is in you will ever be put to shame, but they will be put to shame who are treacherous without excuse.

My third-grade teacher was special. Miss Reeves was kind, caring and gentle. When she discovered that I had a temperature, she drove me home during her lunch break. Miss Reeves also brought make-up work to my home when my bronchitis kept me home for two weeks. She was just that kind of a teacher; she made me want to be just like her.

Catching up after missing ten days of school during my third grade was quite a challenge. On my first day back, our class walked to the auditorium to practice for the program with the other elementary students. During my extended illness at home, the whole school worked on Christmas songs for the parents' program. The students sang energetically through the practice, but I stood quietly wishing I had some words to read so I could sing. Mrs. T. walked up and down the aisle looking for students who were goofing off. She discovered I wasn't singing and grabbed me by the arm. After yanking me to the front of the auditorium, she stopped the singing and announced to the entire school. "This girl thinks she's too good to sing, so she'll spend the rest of the period with her nose in the corner."

I stood in the corner motionless; my heart was breaking. My cheeks were hot, and I fought back the tears. Practice ended, and my teacher returned. She spotted me in the corner and came to check on me. As I tried to tell her what happened, I began to sob. I was so embarrassed, so rejected, and so glad to see my teacher. Miss Reeves took me out of the room and held me for a second and assured me everything was okay. She said she would talk with Mrs. T. That's been years ago, but I can still feel the shame of that moment. Although I have forgiven Mrs. T., my memories of her have never been positive.

Unfortunately, I meet teachers from time to time who believe embarrassing students is a useful form of control for their classrooms. Children are precious in God's sight. Be careful not to offend them. Shame is never an excuse for discipline. Discipline is for correction and instruction. Mrs. T. was not concerned about helping me become a better person. She did not involve herself in building my character. Instead, she used me to intimidate other students who might dare defy her by not singing. Her discipline was not done with love but rather with self-serving anger. I will always be grateful for Miss Reeves who saved me from the teacher who seemed like the "wicked witch" I read about in so many of the children's stories.

Dear God, Give me sensitivity, grace, gentleness, and love when I discipline. Protect me from making harsh decisions that may leave lasting wounds. I want to reflect the love of God each time I discipline my students.

29 OUT OF CONTROL? BEGIN AGAIN

Proverbs 29:19 *Servants cannot be corrected by mere words; though they understand, they will not respond.*

Students tend to test boundaries. They respond to rules that are consistently applied. A classroom rule that is occasionally enforced and ignored at other times is no longer a rule. The rule becomes merely a suggestion. To the student, a suggestion should not have consequences. Any teacher giving discipline for a poorly enforced rule will be accused of unfair discipline practices. A student who receives discipline for a poorly enforced rule will feel picked on and singled out. They will rarely be cooperative and choose to change.

You can begin again at any day and any time of the year. This is done by first admitting to yourself and to your students that you have failed to follow the rules. Next, you review the rules with your students and give them a heads-up that you will be following the rules from that day and every day following. The students will understand your message. They will respect you for your desire to get things right if you take the full responsibility. However, it is imperative that you become consistent in your discipline as you move forward. Students will not tolerate you beginning over and over again.

Dear God, Teach me consistency in discipline. Help me to be sensitive to each situation, but also let me be faithful to apply the school rules in such a way that peace and cooperation are maintained in my classroom. Thank you for inviting me to ask for wisdom. I need your wisdom in this area.

30 CONTEMPT FOR LEADERSHIP BRINGS DESTRUCTION

Deuteronomy 17: 9-13 Go . . . to the judge who is in office at that time. Inquire of them and they will give you the verdict. [10]You must act according to the decisions they give you . . . Be careful to do everything they direct you to do. [11]Act according to the law they teach you and the decisions they give you. Do not turn aside from what they tell you, to the right or to the left. ^{12}*The man who shows contempt for the judge or for the priest who stands ministering there to the LORD your God must be put to death. You must purge the evil from Israel.* ^{13}*All the people will hear and be afraid, and will not be contemptuous again.*

The school year got off to a relatively smooth start, but there were "rumbles" in a particular group. The root of the problem was not evident, but the teachers could sense the antagonism growing within this grade level. As the principal, I invited individual students into my office to get to the root cause of the division. The only thing I saw in common during these interviews were complaints about the rules. It didn't make sense. Many of these students had been in the school the year before, and some had been there for several years without complaint. The rules had not changed for ten years. Why were they angry now?

The anger continued to grow, and I continued dealing with problems without discovering the root cause. One morning I did homeroom for a teacher that was running late. I started the class by taking the role, saying the pledges, taking prayer requests and leading prayer. I felt stiffness among the students and detected several muffled snickers. I sensed a mockery toward the pledges and the prayer time. I secretly felt some pity for the homeroom teacher who had to deal with this attitude on a daily basis. Later, I encouraged the teacher to address the students' negative attitudes and to work toward helping them accept the school policies and procedures.

In April, as I was working with the entire high school on a project, some students came and asked if they could talk with me. Of course, I was always willing to discuss problems with students, but I wasn't prepared for their comments. They began to tell me how angry they were with their homeroom teacher. They said the class never followed homeroom procedures unless

I came through the hallway. They shared several other "secrets" they had kept with that teacher. The teacher had become overly "chummy" with the students and allowed them certain privileges that were against school policies. They thought the teacher was really "cool," and they loved getting around the rules—until the teacher decided to enforce the rules because the students were out of control. When the teacher made them mad, they had ammunition to use against her, and they used it. They enjoyed giving the reports that would get their teacher in trouble.

Unfortunately, the teacher chose to join the wrong team. The teaching staff worked together by supporting one another and maintaining consistency from class to class. This teamwork offered security and clarity to the students as they moved from one teacher to another. However, this one teacher chose to join the students rather than the staff. It created discourse for the entire school. The attitudes of these homeroom students sprinkled throughout the high school as the students moved through their daily schedules. In the end, the teacher learned that students would only be on your team if you do things their way. Once you set some boundaries, they will see what you really are, "one of them," a teacher.

The above Scripture states the importance of following the edicts given by higher authorities. In fact, those who do not support the guidelines laid out for them were considered a grave threat to their nation--so much so that they were instructed to destroy the rebels. When students rebel, they must be corrected. But when a teacher walks in rebellion, it brings destruction to the entire organization. It creates a breakdown in the system.

If you find yourself not wanting to follow your administration—if you cannot come into agreement with your leaders, you should resign your position and seek another job. Think about it! They pay you to follow their leadership—not to make up your own rules. They give you money to do what they feel is essential to their goals and priorities. Your job is to follow. If you cannot follow, don't take the paycheck. Above all, don't rebel against your authorities. Re-read the scripture above to see why this is such an important issue to consider.

Dear God, Wipe away every spot of rebellion from my heart. Help me to understand your truth concerning obedience and yielding to directives. Forgive me for not following my leaders wholeheartedly. I confess pride and arrogance in my "know it all" attitude. I want to start new today with a commitment to follow instructions completely.

31 THERE IS POWER IN GOD'S PRESENCE

2 Thessalonians 1:11-12 With this in mind, we constantly pray for you, that our God may count you worthy of his calling, and that by his power he may fulfill every good purpose of yours and every act prompted by your faith. ¹²We pray this so that the name of our Lord Jesus may be glorified in you, and you in him, according to the grace of our God and the Lord Jesus Christ.

Most Christians experience times when we feel powerless. Difficult discipline issues with no apparent solutions bring discouragement. The balance of home and work duties can defeat us. Relationship problems that seem to be unending can drain us of our energy. And, a personal weakness in self-control can overwhelm us. No matter what your struggle, I want to remind you that there is power in the presence of God. Run to the Rock that is Higher than you, Christ Jesus (Psalm 61:2).

Prayer can change darkness into light, doubt into confidence, and fear into strength. Never underestimate the power of God's presence. As you come into his sanctuary through praise and prayer, you will find rest. God can give you peace that passes all understanding. God can bring clarity of thought. He offers you his wisdom in place of your confusion. The Holy Spirit provides emotional as well as physical healing. He wants to be your All In All.

Know your thoughts. Are they from God? Are they from Satan? Are they old tapes from your past that keep pushing you down? You can bring these thoughts to the altar of God and leave them there. Take captive every defeating thought. Believe the truth and reject the lies. You can exchange God's promises for your hopelessness. As long as there is life, there is hope.

Let God bring light to your situation today. He not only understands your pain; He also offers the complete healing of your person. You can run to him in seconds. It doesn't take hours. Just call out His name. He's been there all the time—waiting for you to call. He loves you with an everlasting love.

Dear God, I am struggling today. Bring your light and your truth to me. I choose to forgive those who treated me wrong. Help me to see how I can make right any wrong I have done. Give me your oil of joy for today. I thank you for your faithfulness and unfailing love.

32 TEACH THEM TO BE WILLING

Isaiah 1:19 "If you are willing and obedient, you will eat the best from the land;"

His teacher said, "Johnny, I must insist that you put away your art tools and come into the reading circle." (Can you feel Johnny's inner struggle? It is apparent that he is not finished with his project.) Finally, kicking his chair and mumbling under his breath, Johnny takes his seat in the reading circle. He obeys, but his heart is not willing. Teachers see this scenario several times a week. Obedience is not easy. Willing obedience is even more difficult.

In Psalm 51, David prays a prayer of repentance asking for a clean heart and a renewed spirit. He wrote, "Restore to me the joy of your salvation and grant me a willing spirit, to sustain me" (Psalm 51:12). Why does David ask for a willing spirit? He knows it will sustain him. David is asking God to protect him from stubborn self-will that leads to rebellion. He wants to follow willingly with a joyful heart rather than grudgingly obeying because of duty. David knows that God has the sustaining power to keep his heart pliable and teachable through conflicts. Through painful experiences, he has learned that the Spirit of God is the only one that can change a rebel into a follower.

Did you fully grasp that last statement? Only God can change a rebel into a follower! A follower is more than someone who obeys the rules or does what he is asked. He takes instruction into his heart, changes his path, and chooses to become like his teacher (Luke 6:42).

Don't forget to address heart issues when you train your students. What's going on in the inside of the child is more important than what shows in the outward behavior. Teach your students the value of "willing" obedience. Isaiah 1:19 and Psalm 51:12 tell us that a willing heart brings joy, sustains life, and allows you to have the "best" in life. We must be willing to become willing. By giving up our stubbornness--by taking a deep breath and letting go of "our way," we submit our hearts to God. When we submit, God can give us the willing heart that leads us to obedient actions.

You cannot make your students willingly obey. Only God can deal with heart issues. However, you can appeal to them and instruct them in the way of a "willing heart." They need to understand what is happening in their own heart. The more they gain understanding on how to deal with their own stubbornness, the sooner they will submit to your leadership. This will help them find contentment and success.

Dear God, Give me a willing heart to follow you and your precepts. Create willing obedience in my own life as I commit to teaching my students willing obedience. Even as Jesus prayed in the Garden of Gesthamane, I pray, "not my will, but yours. . ." (Luke 22:42).

33 DISCIPLINE IS A TOUGH ISSUE

Hebrews 12:5 "...'My son, do not make light of the Lord's discipline and do not lose heart when he rebukes you, ⁶because the Lord disciplines those he loves,   and he punishes everyone he accepts as a son.' ⁷Endure hardship as discipline; God is treating you as sons. For what son is not disciplined by his father? ⁸If you are not disciplined (and everyone undergoes discipline), then you are illegitimate children and not true sons. ⁹Moreover, we have all had human fathers who disciplined us and we respected them for it. How much more should we submit to the Father of our spirits and live! ¹⁰Our fathers disciplined us for a little while as they thought best; but God disciplines us for our good, that we may share in his holiness. ¹¹No discipline seems pleasant at the time, but painful. Later on, however, it produces a harvest of righteousness and peace for those who have been trained by it."

Many controversies exist regarding the appropriate way to discipline children. Some feel that distractions, timeouts, discussions, and coercion through reasoning work best. Others follow Solomon's teachings in Proverbs regarding physical punishment. Others ascribe to Jesus' words on sowing and reaping by supporting the concept of tough love. Many child specialists refer to physical punishment as child abuse, while others are toughening their perspective on boundaries and the need for consequences to infractions. There are so many ideas; parents hear so many differing opinions. It can feel like we live in a world gone mad. There seems to be little agreement on many different issues including the guidelines for discipline in the home, in the school, in the workplace and in society as a whole. At times, the children seem to be in control instead of the adults. Discipline can undoubtedly be a tough call for teachers.

According to verse 9 in Hebrews 12, children respect those that discipline them. Although they seldom admit it, children and teens desire to be protected and to be trained in right behavior; they need someone to be robust enough to be their leader. They feel secure with boundaries. In fact, students will continue to push you until you make them behave. Then they will settle down and learn. When a teacher sets limits in the classroom that include consequences for disobedience, it sets up a wall of protection for students. Fences are not for punishment, but rather for safety. When children are very young, mothers use playpens and gates to limit their child's accessible space. As children mature, they are given more freedom. This expansion of privilege continues throughout childhood as the child demonstrates the ability and responsibility to handle more freedom.

I believe that limitations are acts of love. Tough love gives consequences and removes privileges when the child shows irresponsibility. Tough love teaches children the balance of privilege and responsibility. It is a fact of life that you lose jobs if you are not responsible. Students build responsibility as they mature and grow in character through the things experienced during childhood. If a child is always protected from pain and never allowed to reap consequences for bad decisions, he will develop a warped perspective of reality. If we fail to discipline him, when he becomes an adult, the world will teach him through rejection and negative consequences. The world is not gentle. These lessons will be painful, if not destructive. Either way, the child or the adult child will reap consequences.

Galatians 6:7 says "Do not be deceived: God cannot be mocked. A man reaps what he sows."

Discipline, though painful for the moment, produces good fruit. As adults, we must look past the pain, anger, resentment, and rebellion of the student to the good things he will gain because of his suffering. It is more loving to allow limited suffering in their childhood than to produce a dysfunctional adult that is unable to deal with the pressures of the adult world. Independence, self-discipline, and confidence are our ultimate goal for each child. These traits develop as the child discovers his ability to control himself, to do right, and to gain acceptance through correct behavior.

I do not encourage teachers to use corporal punishment, but I do believe there may be times that parents may need a mild form of discipline. Adults should use consequences that fit the crime. For instance, if a student writes on the desk, he can clean student desks to gain respect for school property. If a student creates arguments on the playground, he should not go to the playground the next recess. If he repeats the disturbance on the playground, he should receive a more extended period of time-out. I could go on and on listing consequences, but the important thing is that you know what the consequences will be ahead of time and that you are consistent to give the same result to each infraction according to the severity of the behavior.

Discipline should be unpleasant. When the pain (unpleasantness, disappointment, restrictions, loss of privileges, etc.) to stay the way you are is worse than the pain it takes to change, then a child will change. For most of us, it requires pain to bring positive change in our lives. It is tough to inflict pain on someone you love, but seeing beyond his or her present pain to the character they will gain, can make us willing to suffer through the discipline process with our students.

Dear God, Even as you discipline me and allow me to suffer consequences of my actions, give me the courage to train my students by giving them the consequences they have earned. Let me love them enough to discipline them consistently.

34 HOLD ON TO COURAGE AND HOPE

Hebrews 3:6-11 *But Christ is faithful as a son over God's house. And we are his house, if we hold on to our courage and the hope of which we boast. [7]So, as the Holy Spirit says: "Today, if you hear his voice, [8]do not harden your hearts as you did in the rebellion, during the time of testing in the desert,...[10]That is why I was angry with that generation, and I said, `Their hearts are always going astray, and they have not known my ways.'[11]So I declared on oath in my anger, `They shall never enter my rest.' "*

Life is tough. The older I become, the more I know there are very few "storybook" endings. However, I also have lived long enough to see bad things become stepping stones toward good changes in me. The briar and the rose often are used in literature to represent life experiences. Good things mixed with the hurt, pain, and disappointment help us grow in character. Without the thorns and the pain, few of us would ever bloom into the lovely rose that God designed us to become.

Life brings pain automatically. Ecclesiastes 9:11 says that "... time and chance happen to them all." Becoming a victim, whether of a perpetrator, a misunderstanding, or a situation out of our control, happens to most of us in varying degrees. Very few escape victimization of some kind. Therefore, the questions are not just "How do we avoid being victimized," but even more importantly, "How do we overcome victimization?"

God has given us promises in the Bible that offers courage and hope. We are told how God is intimately involved with the details of our lives. He even knows when the common sparrow falls. But we have the choice to believe God's report or not to believe it. Our decisions will make a difference in our healing process. What we choose will make a difference in our moving forward or digging a deeper pit as we go in circles seeking our own answers. Without courage and hope, we wander aimlessly like the Children of Israel in the desert never really going forward and never finding our promised rest.

The Spirit of God stands beside you to offer you courage and hope; forces of darkness may be offering you reasons to blame God and others for your crisis. The way you handle those accusations will affect your future. The Children of Israel kept choosing unbelief, fear, doubt, and anger toward God and the leader He gave them. They believed the false report. They lost their courage and hope, and they never saw the promised land. They never entered into the joy that God had set before them.

Seek to find the sunshine in every rain cloud. Look for blessing when it looks like a curse. Remember, that in God's timing, He can and will make all things beautiful if you will cling to courage and hope in Christ!

Dear God, Forgive me when I falter in my faith in you. I want to follow you no matter what trouble comes my way. I know I can trust you in the hardest of circumstances because you are God!

35 PRAYER IS YOUR LIFELINE

Matthew 26:40-41 *Then he returned to his disciples and found them sleeping. "Could you men not keep watch with me for one hour?" he asked Peter. *^{41}*"Watch and pray so that you will not fall into temptation. The spirit is willing, but the body is weak."*

As Jesus faced the final test of his earthly ministry—the crucifixion, he turned to fervent prayer with his Heavenly Father for strength and comfort. He understood that prayer is where battles are won! Jesus overcame the cross in the Garden of Gethsemane! During the long hours of prayer, he died to his human emotions and fears. He chose prayer over food, sleep, fellowship, and even ministering to those in need. It was his connection to God's power that allowed Him to overcome the flesh. He did not neglect prayer. He denied His flesh and kept it under subjection by denying it the right to rule. He crucified himself through prayer before the soldiers ever came to take him away! He endured the cross because he died in the garden before he walked to Calvary. He was a walking dead man. He was wholly surrendered to God's will.

Let us strive to keep watch in prayer for the needs that surround us at school. We must understand that our battles are spiritual and not physical. We fight against powers and principalities—not coworkers, parents, or students. May we never become weary of doing what is right. May we never allow our prayer life to take second place to ministry. Prayer is your lifeline to the overcoming power needed to face challenging tasks today. Pray first!

Dear God, Forgive me for not praying enough. Help me to realize more fully how important you are to every part of my life. I want to take you with me everywhere I go rather than just talk with you a few minutes every morning. Let my life become a prayer to you as I move throughout my day.

36 OBEDIENCE IS FOUNDATIONAL FOR TRUE WORSHIP

I Samuel 15:22 *Samuel replied, "Does the LORD delight in burnt offerings and sacrifices as much as in obeying the LORD? To obey is better than sacrifice, and to heed is better than the fat of rams."*

King Saul was instructed by Samuel, the prophet, to destroy Israel's enemy, the Amalekites, and everything they owned. I Samuel 15:9 reported, *But Saul and the army spared Agag and the best of the sheep and cattle, the fat calves[b] and lambs—everything that was good. These they were unwilling to destroy completely, but everything that was despised and weak they utterly destroyed.* As a result of his incomplete disobedience, Saul lost God's favor and his kingdom.

Obedience is foundational to God's blessings. It is our highest act of worship. God seeks obedience over repentance. I once heard an educator explain his rationale for not following his principal's directive with this statement--"It is easier to get forgiveness than permission." It was his way of dealing with rules he felt were unfair or wrong. That phrase would have fit Saul's position perfectly, but God didn't respond to his disobedience lightly. Saul was guilty of purposeful disobedience often called "incomplete" obedience.

Jesus said in John 14:23 *...Anyone who loves me will obey my teaching. My Father will love them, and we will come to them and make our home with them.*

Obedience is foundational to building character. Are we teaching children the value of obedience? Have we learned the importance of obedience? Jesus gives us a great example from his own life. When he was twelve years old, his parents became upset with him for not letting them know where he was. His response to them was submission and obedience. In Luke 1:51-52, we read where Jesus obeyed his earthly parents and "grew in wisdom and stature, and in favor with God and man." If Jesus, the Son of God, submitted to human authority, should we, as teachers, and our students not also learn the same response?

Dear God, My heart longs to love and worship you. Help me to choose to obey my leaders as an act of my worship to you. Give me direction on how to instill the value of obeying to my students. Modern culture continues to grow more defiant and rebellious toward authority. Give me a greater understanding of your ways and teach me to follow you in complete obedience.

(Thank you, Dr. John D. Barge, Georgia State School Superintendent, 2016, for the inspiration for this devotion.)

37 I NEED YOUR FORGIVENESS

Matthew 6:14-15 *For if you forgive men when they sin against you, your heavenly Father will also forgive you. ^{15}But if you do not forgive men their sins, your Father will not forgive your sins.*

Matthew 18:32-34 *"Then the master called the servant in. `You wicked servant,' he said, `I canceled all that debt of yours because you begged me to. ^{33}Shouldn't you have had mercy on your fellow servant just as I had on you?' ^{34}In anger his master turned him over to the jailers to be tortured until he should pay back all he owed.*

Matthew 18:35 *This is how my heavenly Father will treat each of you unless you forgive your brother from your heart.*

When I know someone is angry with me, I hurt inside. And, when I am wrong, I might as well admit it because it will bother me until I confess and make it right. Having Christ in my life has made me sensitive to my need for forgiveness. Not only do I have a need to forgive others and to be forgiven, so do all the people who offended me.

When should I forgive someone for doing something against me? Is it after I have punished them enough or after they have apologized in the right way or when I decide that they really understand what they did to me? How do I want God to respond to my request for forgiveness? Is it after I have been punished enough, or after I learn to apologize and repent in the right way or when I decide that I really understand what I did wrong? Since God freely forgives us each time we ask for forgiveness, we must also work toward forgiveness of our fellowman even when we feel they don't deserve to be forgiven.

Forgiveness is a process. Keep forgiving--over and over again--until God does the work in your heart, and the pain goes away. Holding on to your offense and refusing to forgive makes you a prisoner of your offender. You will be unable to move forward in your life until you release the one who hurt you--even when they don't deserve it or don't ask to be forgiven. When you cut off your love for another person, you become incapable of receiving love from anyone. Trust God enough to open your heart once again to love, to believe, to forgive, and to release those who hurt you. If you forgive, you will feel ten pounds lighter, the birds will sing again, and the sunshine will bring courage and hope to give you a brighter future.

Good people do bad things. Sometimes the mistakes they make are terrible, but God can restore and make things new again if we will take our brokenness to him and ask him to fix it. Give yourself time to heal. God can forgive instantly, but, for us, it takes time. We must be willing to forgive over and over again until the pain eventually fades.

How long will you keep yourself a prisoner of unforgiveness and anger? How long will you choose bondage over freedom? Make it a habit to forgive yourself and to forgive others—again and again until the pain is gone.

Dear God, I hurt! I want to want to forgive, but I don't have the desire right now. Help me to be willing to forgive. Help me to remember the times that I have wronged others and the sins I have committed before you. Help me to appreciate the forgiveness you have given me. Give me the courage to forgive others because you continue to forgive me.

38 PAIN CAN BE A BLESSING

Proverbs 27:6 *Wounds from a friend can be trusted, but an enemy multiplies kisses.*

Have you learned to praise God for emotional pain caused by someone's attack? If not, you probably have not worked through the issue enough. What do I mean? When you are wounded, search through the offense and ask yourself why it hurt? What about the offense caused you so much pain?

It was a letter from a friend. The letter was not angry or attacking, but it was full of my friend's feelings and pain. My friend listed specific details describing how I hurt and rejected them. My friend clearly described things in me that caused them not to trust me anymore and made it hard to remain my friend. I felt crushed. I cried. I prayed. I waited for answers.

This letter attacked the most vulnerable areas of my life. It named faults that I felt were unchangeable and hopeless. It named my besetting sins. It required me to face myself squarely and see what was wrong. I knew I was against a wall. Only God could change me in these areas. No amount of self-control or strong-will would do it. I had tried that. I wept in despair, feeling there was no way out of the pit. I was helpless, hopeless, and unchangeable.

But God . . . Yes, what a wonderful phrase. God began to bring light into my darkness. I started discovering lies planted in my subconscious years earlier about who I was and who I could not be. God brought truth to those lies and began to set me free.

God pierced my heart with the revelation of my own sin -- not to hurt me but to set me free. Without the deep pain, I would never have had the courage to search for the root cause of the sin. I would not have discovered and dealt with the "lies."

I continue to climb the mountain to victory over these areas of weaknesses, but now I can see some light. I am going forward, PTL! I now know the truth, and the truth is setting me free. Thank you, Lord, for faithful friends who are willing to speak the truth in love even when it wounds. Surgery hurts for a season, but it brings wholeness and health. The pain only lasts for a time.

You too may believe a lie about your besetting sin. Be willing to allow God to reveal the truth to your heart. Allow him to do surgery and begin to remove the lies and wrong concepts that keep you in bondage. When the truth comes, freedom from the sin will begin to manifest. It often takes pain to change. Learn to praise God for your pain.

Dear God, Thank you for cleansing pain. Help me always to remain teachable. I open my heart to you today! Reveal sinful roots in me; convict my heart. Bring me to the light of your truth so I can be set free.

39 WHAT GOES AROUND COMES AROUND!

Ecclesiastes 1:9 "What has been will be again, what has been done will be done again; there is nothing new under the sun."

When the teacher entered the room, I could tell she was upset. "I'm so sorry, Mrs. Wyrick," she said. I didn't want you to see this note I took from a student. I talked with the principal about it, and he told me to give it to you. He felt that you would know what to do with it." I looked at her puzzled as she continued. "It says some really nasty things about you. I told the principal that I thought the girl ought to be kicked out for writing that kind of a note about a teacher. I'm sorry you have to read it, but here it is."

She stood and watched me as I read the note. She was right; it was awful. Under my breath, I prayed for wisdom. Instantly, God reminded me of a similar incident when I was in the eighth grade. It was strange; this girl was in the eighth grade too. I knew what I was to do. I thanked the teacher for bringing me the note, and I told her that I would speak with the student.

My friend and I loved to write each other notes. They were usually unimportant, rambling words--much about nothing. One day I was frustrated with my choir teacher because he kept treating our choir class like a sing-a-long instead of an actual choir. I spewed my thoughts and feelings out on notebook paper both front and back during one of my classes and included several unkind descriptions of the teacher. I was not so much upset with my teacher as I was ranting for the sake of writing an exciting note to my friend. The things I said in the letter were not untruthful, but it expressed more disdain for my teacher than I really felt.

Since I would see my friend right after choir, I carried the note unfolded on top of my books as I left the classroom. My teacher stood at the classroom door as we left; he saw the note. He snatched it and said, "Oh, Elderine, is this a note?"

I panicked. I grabbed the note and wrestled for it. The note tore, and I got half of it. Unfortunately, the teacher got the wrong half. Most of the ugly words I had written about him were in his hands. He read it. Then he said, "Young lady, you need to talk to me before you leave."

My heart pounded. I did like my teacher. I was just writing; it was just something to write. Oh, if I had not written all those things down. I knew I was in trouble. I sat and waited until the other students left. Then the teacher sat down on his stool and faced me. He looked at me a second and then asked me to explain what I meant in the note. I did. I also told him that I liked him as a teacher, but I would prefer to have choir class rather than a sing-a-long.

He listened quietly for a few minutes then he said, "Elderine, I'm going to overlook this note. But let me give you some advice. Never write anything down that you don't want others to read." (I can assure you that I never forgot that advice.) He let me know that the incident was finished, and he allowed me to leave.

And sixteen years later, I was about to face a student over a similar issue. I had a mixture of mercy and grace in my heart for her. I knew how she felt. I understood because I had been there. When we met, we talked; I shared my note story; I forgave her; I found out what was bothering her, and I prayed with her about her problems at home and at school. We hugged each other, and I sent her on her way without consequences showing the same mercy that my teacher showed me. I am still friends with this young lady and her family today.

Teachers, do not forget what it was like to be a kid. Love them in spite of their foolishness.

Dear God, Thank you for preparing me for this situation sixteen years earlier. Thank you for giving me a wise choir teacher who saw beyond my foolishness into my heart. Your ways are beyond description.'

40 FAVORITISM BRINGS TROUBLE

Genesis 37:3-4 *Now Israel loved Joseph more than any of his other sons, because he had been born to him in his old age; and he made a richly ornamented robe for him. ⁴When his brothers saw that their father loved him more than any of them, they hated him and could not speak a kind word to him.*

Favoritism occurs throughout the book of Genesis. Isaac was favored over Ishmael. Then Isaac preferred his oldest son, Esau and Rebecca preferred the youngest boy, Jacob (Genesis 15:27-28). Jacob later is forced to marry Leah before he can marry Rachel (his true love). He showed preference to Rachel (Genesis 29:28-30). Jacob also showed an open display of favoritism toward Joseph over his other brothers by giving him a colorful coat.

In each case, there were prices paid for this preferential treatment. Again and again, hard feelings developed. Isaac's sons never learned to honor each other. His youngest son deceived Jacob and stole his brother's birthright and then fled for his life. He stayed in another land for several years for safety. Leah, the wife Jacob did not choose, spent her entire life having children for Jacob trying to gain his approval (which she never did). Leah's unhappiness and desire to be loved can easily be seen through the meaning of names she gave her children-- Reuben (the Lord has seen my misery--Gen 29:28); Simeon (because the Lord heard that I am not loved--Gen. 29:33); Levi (at last my husband will become attached to me--Gen. 29:34); Judah (This time I will praise the Lord--Gen 29:35). Joseph's brothers hated him because of his unique treatment which resulted in them selling him into slavery. The brothers allowed their father to believe that Joseph was killed by an animal.

When a teacher favors a student, the entire class will reject that student. They will also become furious with the teacher. It is natural for some personalities to be more appealing to us than others, but we must consciously work at not preferring one student over another. The fruit that comes from such seeds is destructive. If you hear a student accuse you of having a teacher's pet, do not take it lightly. You may be preferring students without your realizing it. Check your heart and your actions.

One way to avoid this pitfall is to determine in your heart to involve each student in your discussion and times of participation. Methodically keep a mental check to make sure that even the quietest, uninvolved student is encouraged to perform. You will build a relationship with your entire class as you make it a point to be aware of each student every day.

Dear God, Each student is fearfully and wonderfully made by you. Help me to see the "uniqueness" of each child. Alert me to any favoritism in my life and give me the wisdom to avoid this pitfall.

41 DO THEY HAVE A WILLING SPIRIT?

Psalm 51:12 *Restore to me the joy of your salvation and grant me a willing spirit, to sustain me.*

Obedience is imperative; we must train students to obey. But are we teaching teachers and students the value of a willing heart? Isaiah 1:19 says "If you are willing and obedient, you will eat the best from the land." Learning to obey from the heart is a valuable part of building character. Yielding my will to follow someone else's priority is a necessary part of becoming a socially responsible citizen.

Willingness develops inwardly. The mind, the will, and the emotions work together to bring a child into "true submission." The word submission does not mean "slavery." It refers to a willingness to follow. One of the obvious differences in a child and an adult is that an adult has learned (hopefully) when to lead and when to follow, when to stand their ground and not give in and when to release their own ideas and follow someone else for the good of the whole group. The character trait of "willingness" involves being able to turn away from self-centeredness to make a responsible choice of action that brings the best good for the situation.

When we train obedience, let us also teach about developing a willing heart. This does not mean blind obedience, but a responsible choice made from the heart and mind because you understand that the decision is the right thing to do. The Bible speaks of areas where a "willing heart" is needed. If interested in a deeper understanding of willingness, check out these scriptures:
- Willing to follow Christ (Matt. 4:19)
- Willing to praise (God and others) Ps. 119:108
- Willing to obey Isaiah 1:19
- Willing to listen Ezekiel 3:7
- Willing to share I Timothy 6:18
- Willing to serve God and others I Peter 5:2
- Willing to die to your own will if God requires it Luke 22:42

Dear God, Develop a willing heart in me. Give me a greater understanding of heart issues that so often affect my outward responses. I submit my heart to you for examination and change. Give me a willing heart, O Lord.

42 DON'T FORGET TO HAVE FUN!

Proverbs 17:22 *A merry heart doeth good like a medicine but a broken spirit drieth the bones.* KJV

You can affect your health in more ways than diet, nutrition, exercise, and sleep. Your attitude and outlook on life affect your health. A cheerful outlook on life helps us to face life's ups and downs. We all have them, but how you deal with them makes a difference.

How long has it been since you met with a friend or a group of friends to have fun and no other reason? Summer is a great time for backyard activities like volleyball, baseball, horseshoes, croquet, bocce balls, bean toss, washers, and other games. I have great memories of having family and friends over to make homemade ice cream with games of horseshoes and croquet in our backyard. Other times it was hot dogs with watermelon. Or perhaps you prefer having guests over for dinner or a church social. People enrich our lives. Have you discovered the joy of fellowship?

As Christians, we are instructed to rejoice. "Rejoice in the Lord always ..." Phil 4:4. We need to learn to be content with what we have. Discontentment will ruin our health. I Timothy 6:6 reminds us that success is being able to be satisfied, living right, and pleasing God. Determine to be joyful, loving, thankful, peaceful, forgiving, and grateful. Do something unexpected for someone without expecting something in return. Decide to be aware of your fun time this year. If you do, you will feel more rested and revived for the next school year.

The adage, "All work and no play makes _____ a dull (boy/girl).' What about it? Are you ready to do something fun this year?

Dear God, I need to relax more and enjoy this school year, especially the school breaks. Give me the wisdom and determination to find that place of contentment, and enjoyment with my family and friends. I ask you to give me a merry heart that enjoys being with others and can bless others. Amen.

43 I CHOOSE TO TRUST YOU IN THIS TRIAL

Proverbs 3:5-6(KJV) *Trust in the L*ORD *with all thine heart; and lean not unto thine own understanding.*[6] *In all thy ways acknowledge him, and he shall direct thy paths.*

Every school year can bring changes, frustrations, disappointments, and conflict. Teachers can become anxious about the tasks ahead and worry about problems that seem to be waiting around the corner. Slow down; breathe deeply; turn your thoughts toward eternal things. Set aside your concerns about today.

Remind yourself that God can be trusted. Anytime, anywhere, in all circumstances, God is in control. Are you facing things that seem impossible? Are you having a difficult time seeing God's plan or provision in your life today? Don't rely on your feelings or your understanding. Turn to the Word of God—"I am the Truth, the Life, the Way." His Word says, "I will never leave you nor forsake you. Lo, I am with you always, even to the end of the age." (John 14:5; Matthew 28:20).

You may not feel God's presence, but He is there. You may not see His hand, but He is carrying you. Acknowledge God as the ultimate, sovereign Father who only does good—not evil. He can take your ashes and replace them with beauty (Isaiah 61:3). He can restore what Satan destroys. He does make all things beautiful in His time!

Trust Jesus and learn to be content right now. He is your Shelter. Run into His truth today and be healed of your doubt, your frustration, and your unrest. He is our Peace who has broken down every wall. Learn to lean on Christ, our solid Rock.

Take one step at a time toward completing the insurmountable tasks before you. Remember to pray for those who irritate you or have disagreements with you. Submit yourself to the authority God has placed over you. Bless each person on your team. Trust God to smooth things out as you submit to HIS WILL.

Dear God, I want to trust you more. Help me to find my way out of the stinking thinking that comes from trouble and into a level of faith and trust that pleases you. I want to know your ways more. Deep in my heart, I realize that you do all things well and that you are directing my path today. I choose to rest in your promises.

44 CALLED TO MAKE A DIFFERENCE

Deuteronomy 12:28 Be careful to obey all these regulations I am giving you, so that it may always go well with you and your children after you, because you will be doing what is good and right in the eyes of the Lord your God.

Are you overlooking the less spectacular issues, the little things in your life that have the power to make a difference—negative or positive? Are there secret areas of your life where you fail to do right that affects your influence? These hidden flaws can pull the plug in the difference God wanted to make in your life. Your actions will bring a blessing or harm to the children under your care.

Samson was called from birth to be a man of God (Judges 13:2-5; 16:20-21). He was called to be bring deliverance to Israel, but he was proud, ignored his parent's instruction, and chose the wrong friends. His ungodly girlfriend tricked him into revealing the secret of his strength. He was attacked, had his eyes gouged out and was sent to prison. This was not his difference that God intended. His difference was minimized because of his wrong choices.

There were three lessons that Samson hadn't learned that kept God from using him to the extent that God wanted to use him. I encourage you to teach these valuable lessons to your students. Samson ...

REJECTED COUNCIL—Samson's parents warned him about his friends (women), but he didn't listen. He rejected his parent's boundaries.

LACKED SELF-CONTROL—Samson refused to control his fleshly desires. Uncontrolled desires lead to destruction. These indulgences cost Samson more than he was expecting. They shortened his life and diminished his purposes. It was not circumstances, not godless governments, not other people that destroyed him; it was his own desires that brought him down. Our culture encourages such indulgences. These indulgences cost more than he ever wanted to pay. God established guidelines for expressing our physical desires. There are safety, freedom and protection within God's guidelines.

DIDN'T LEARN FROM HIS MISTAKES—Samson continued to make the same mistakes with women over and over again. We are human, and humans make mistakes, but to be successful in our purpose, we must evaluate our mistakes and determine how to avoid repeating them. When we choose a cycle of destruction, we will eventually be scarred permanently.

All three of these issues are extremely important lessons for today's students. First, as educators and significant role models for our students, we must make sure our lives reflect the wisdom we want to instill in our students. Next, we must find opportunities to teach these principles using current and historical events. You can make a difference by being willing to discuss the need for wisdom and correct choices.

Dear God, I do want to be a difference maker. Give me the wisdom to discover the right time and place for instructions in right choices. Lead me daily as I work to make a difference in my students' lives.

45 A SEASON AND A TIME FOR EVERYTHING

Ecclesiastes 3:2 *A time to plant and a time to pluck up.*

I remember my husband transplanting the small Redbud tree in our front yard. It was such an exciting thing to watch the little sapling take root and begin to flourish. I enjoyed the cute purple blooms in the spring, and the beautiful round leaves in the summer and fall. The tree developed perfectly in the spot next to the street. It became a landmark used to locate our house. My husband and I remarked several times about how pleased we were with our Redbud tree. One day we noticed that the leaves on our tree were wilting. Full limbs were losing their leaves without cause. After inspecting the tree, my husband discovered that someone bored a hole completely through the trunk of our tree. Unfortunately, nothing could be done. Our tree withered and eventually was cut down and discarded. Once where there once was a flourishing tree, now stands a few scraggly limbs working their way up from the roots to remind us what once had been.

As I age, it seems that experiences of decline and loss are becoming more plentiful. Recently, we lost several dear friends in death, churches have closed, businesses have declined, and many around us struggle financially. My question to God becomes, "God how do I respond to so much decline and loss? Where are you in the middle of all the change I see in my life?"

God's quiet, gentle answer is simple. "I am in it all. I promised never to leave you, nor forsake you. Trust me, and keep following me. My way leads to life, not death." Turning to the Scriptures, I was reminded of Elijah who sat by the water brook being fed by the Ravens. His comfort was not to last. One day his water brook dried up, and he was forced to leave. God was moving him forward. His circumstances required the move. God uses circumstances to move us forward toward our next purpose in life. We must not balk; we need to follow God's leading.

In your next crisis or disappointment, seek God's will in the situation. Give God time, and He can make all things beautiful for you. Remember, our joy is not in our circumstances, but it is in knowing Christ. Submitting to God's purposes and His will is the key to contentment and inner peace. God knows the times and the seasons of your life. Trust Him.

Dear God, I often find myself in the state of confusion or disappointment. Teach me to see your Will in the midst of the changing of seasons and in the different times you have ordered for my life. I choose to trust you and follow you unconditionally.

46 ARE YOUR JOKES FUNNY? ARE THEY HURTFUL?

Ephesians 4:29 *Let no corrupt communication proceed out of your mouth, but that which is good to the use of edifying, that it may minister grace unto the hearers. (KJV)*

Ever wondered why so many jokes magnify people's weaknesses rather than their strengths? Students who have not been hardened by the world are like sponges. They believe what they are told about themselves. Elementary and even junior high students will often absorb things said to them and accept it as truth. These early messages from those they trust and love are planted deep into the child's subconscious and create a picture of who they are. Words said in jest may influence a child's hope for the future.

Children who are told they can't learn or told that they are too slow to be good at school will believe that message and become what they believe—a school dropout or a poor student. Children who are made fun of for being fat or clumsy or messy will build that image of themselves and struggle with it all of their lives.

Words that build up are words like, "Wow, I am proud of you. That's really an accomplishment." Words that tear down are like the following zinger I heard at an award ceremony. "Wow, Mike, you are the only boy with a penmanship award. Does that mean that you write like a girl?"

There are websites explicitly dedicated for joke tellers. I found a site is entitled "Zingers—Insults for Every Occasion." It offers a myriad of unkind words that can bring a laugh at others' expense. Although these type of jokes may be entertaining, teachers should not use "zingers" toward any students at any time. Even when a student laughs at a zinger, inside, he may be secretly embarrassed and/or hurt. Our words should edify our students. As professionals, we cannot afford to take the chance of offending a student—even when joking. Jesus said that it is better for us to be drowned in the sea than to offend a child (Matthew 18:6). As teachers who desire to please God in all our ways, we need to ask the Holy Spirit to build sensitivity and gentleness in our communication. An offended student will be less likely to learn in your classroom.

Dear God, Give me wisdom and discernment regarding my words. I ask that you make my heart sensitive to the feelings of my students. "May the words of my mouth... be acceptable in your sight..." Psalm 19:14.

47 IS YOUR SENSE OF DUTY TOO EXTREME?

Ecclesiastes 12:13-14 (KJV) ...*Fear God, and keep his commandments: for this is the whole duty of man. ¹⁴For God shall bring every work into judgment, with every secret thing, whether it be good, or whether it be evil.*

One day, in prayer, I began to feel convicted about my "sense of duty." I considered my responsible attitude and my ability to meet people's expectations to be a positive trait. (In reality, I was driven to meet everyone's demands. I felt guilty when I fell short of anyone's request.) As I meditated on the thought that a sense of duty might be a negative rather than a positive trait, I realized that I was putting the demands of people and projects ahead of my private devotions and my family. The light came on! I realized that my "sense of duty" was out of control. With God's help and my husband's support, I began to evaluate my use of time and commitment to those I served.

Responsibility is a good word, right? I agree that it is good as long as it doesn't cause feelings of guilt, condemnation, and hopelessness. Manipulators readily abuse those who desire to do right. They often ask those with a servant's heart to go the "extra mile" repeatedly. Guilt (or praise) is used to encourage the worker to give more time and service than what is appropriate.

I recently read an article by Bill Puka (2005) in which he compared the word *"responsibility"* to the term "response-ability." He defined **responsibility** as "a felt requirement, a debt owed, usually a burdensome duty ..." In contrast, he defined **response-ability** as "the ability to respond to others ...[which] focuses us on our own worth and the value of our talents or potentials." Response-ability teaches us to be responsible for ourselves, our integrity, and the freedom and the ability to choose to do the right thing for everyone involved. Response-ability encourages the empowerment of the individual rather than forcing a mandated subservient response.

Give this some thought as you teach this year. You can learn to respond correctly to requests. You will find greater joy in serving when you choose your actions based on your freedom to choose. This is also a concept you can teach your students. We all need more response-ability. Knowing we can respond correctly in stressful situations will help to build self-control and self-worth in all of us.

Dear God, Allow me to understand my response-ability regarding my "sense of duty." Help me to see the freedom and peace in understanding the strength and wisdom that your Spirit gives me to choose the best areas of service. Bring balance to my life so that I might run the race set before me without burning out before I reach the finish line.

Work Cited-Puka, B. (2005). *Teaching Ethical Excellence: Artful Response-Ability, Creative Integrity, Character Opus. Liberal Education, 91*(3), 22+. Retrieved November 1, 2009, from Questia database:

http://www.questia.com/ PM.qst?a=o&d=5011979265

48 WHAT DOES THE LORD REQUIRE OF ME?

Micah 6:8 (KJV) *He hath shewed thee, O man, what is good; and what doth the LORD require of thee, but to do justly, and to love mercy, and to walk humbly with thy God?*

According to Micah 6:8 there are three things that God requires of us—(1) To do justly, (2) to love mercy, and (3) to walk humbly with God. Justice means being impartial, fair, and doing what is right. Mercy shows compassion and concern for another. Humility considers the needs of others over our own.

Classroom management is challenging. Teachers often react to classroom situations without considering the justice of their actions. Unfortunately, teachers repeat unjust actions and merciless decisions against students without realizing it.

For instance, if a student turns in his/her math test (or any other test) with unanswered questions, most teachers will quickly place an "X" on the unanswered problems and grade the test. I propose that the love of Christ compels us to ask the student, "John, did you mean to leave these questions blank?" If he says no, the teacher's mercy and love would allow him to complete the problems. Or, perhaps as you grade a paper, you realize the student misread the instructions which caused him to miss every question in that section. Maybe true justice mixed with mercy and humility would compel the teacher to ask the student to do that section again following the correct instructions.

Immediately, some will say that is not right. The student should have caught those mistakes. My question to you is, "What is your purpose for giving a test? Is it to measure the child's learning? If so, how does counting off points for his carelessness measure his true learning?" If grades do not reflect the child's knowledge, they are not accurate measurements of learning. Too many times we use grades to "punish" a student assuming we are training the child by giving a lower grade. Is this type measurement accurate or just? The most important question regarding the Scripture above is, "What is 'good' in this situation?"

As an example, I would like to share a personal experience with you. My dyslexic son was in the third grade. We worked extremely hard every night to get his work completed and to keep his grades up. One morning I checked his backpack and found a large stack of papers. They appeared to be graded and returned by the teacher. In a rush, I removed the papers and placed them on the kitchen table planning to look through them when I returned home. About an hour after school began, my son came rushing to my classroom and asked me where his papers were. He told me that he had a history paper in his backpack that was due that day. I assured him everything would be okay. I would explain to his teacher that it was my fault. To my shock and dismay, the teacher gave my son a "0" for the paper. She said I was asking for special privileges because I was a teacher. I told her that it was my fault, and my son didn't even know that I took the papers out. I told her we would get the paper to her later that afternoon or first thing the next morning. She refused to accept the assignment. She would not even consider my appeal. To this day I cannot see the justice or mercy in her response.

I often hear similar stories from parents. As representatives of Jesus Christ, let us consider decisions through eyes of justice and mercy looking for what is "good" and "best" in the situation. As teachers, let us seek to be a blessing to the children and their parents rather than a stumbling block.

Dear God, Open my heart to understand justice and mercy. I need the mind of Christ to make decisions on an individual basis. Fill me with your wisdom and your grace.

49 OBEDIENCE IS BETTER THAN FORGIVENESS

Proverbs 21:3 To do what is right and just is more acceptable to the LORD than sacrifice.

There are lasting consequences from not following the rules set out by the administration. When the rules are not enforced in one classroom or department, it creates confusion and resentment toward leaders who are following the rules. When you ignore a rule that all of your students understand, students are encouraged to disobey. It essentially negates the rule.

Leaders must not build rebellion in students. If we do not agree with a rule, it is our responsibility to do one of two things. We can make an official appeal to the one that made the rule and try to get the rule changed, or we can follow the rule and encourage the students to learn true obedience as they submit to a rule they don't particularly like.

Obedience is only learned when we obey through suffering. Obedience is giving up our "will" to follow the mandate of a leader, parent, or authority. When students are never challenged to submit to authority; they grow up without putting away the rebellion bound up in their heart (Proverbs 22:15). The Scriptures tell us that even Jesus learned from the things he suffered (Hebrews 5:8). True obedience begins when we obey an authority even when we don't particularly want to do what we are told to do. When we are asked to do something we want to do, we are merely agreeing rather than obeying. Obedience builds strength in character and a commitment to doing what is right.

Dear God, Open my eyes and help me to see if there is any rebellion in my heart toward my leaders. Teach me complete obedience so I might lead my students into a greater commitment to obey God as they obey those in authority over them. Our world is very self-willed and rebellious. Work in my heart to build a greater desire to honor you through obedience to my supervisors.

50 GOD CAN BE TRUSTED IN THE STORM

Matthew 8:23-26 Then he got into the boat and his disciples followed him. Suddenly a furious storm came up on the lake, so that the waves swept over the boat. But Jesus was sleeping. The disciples went and woke him, saying, "Lord, save us! We're going to drown!" He replied, "You of little faith, why are you so afraid?" Then he got up and rebuked the winds and the waves, and it was completely calm.

This has been a week of reflection for me as I celebrate my 50th wedding anniversary. There have been many storms, and many lessons learned over the years. I met my husband at church when I was twelve. Little did I know that this cute, funny young teenage boy would become such a significant influence in my life. Life happens--important things happen--yet often we are unaware of what is transpiring right in the middle of our regular, ordinary, everyday life. God is at work in our lives at all times. He is in control, directing our paths and working things for our good.

I have watched friends and family members work through loss, disappointments, struggles and deal with difficult questions when life doesn't make sense. Many times I see parallels in their circumstances with the ones I have faced in my past. I have learned that life has patterns. There is pain, sorrow, joy, and rewards along the path. Every decision brings a consequence. We can learn by understanding the cause and effect of our choices and the decisions of others. We often have the opportunity to observe other people's failure or success through their trials. Do we have eyes to see and ears to hear? Are we teachable? Do we seek counsel when facing unclear decisions? Do we know where to find counsel? Are we familiar enough with the Bible to apply God's instruction to our dilemma? Is our prayer life current to enable us to hear God's direction?

What does all this have to do with teaching? Everything! Who you are is what will make a difference in your classroom--not just what you do. Students will remember you much longer than they remember your lessons. Allow God to permeate every part of your professional and personal life. Look for his work in all your experiences. His hand is there if you have eyes to see and ears to hear. He will never leave you. He will direct your path. Although He may appear to be uninvolved, He is aware of your storm, and He has it all under control. Trust Him!

Dear God, Thank you for being completely aware of our circumstances and needs today. Help us to trust you more and to lean on your eternal wisdom and guidance. We know that you are good, and you do all things well. Help us to find your will in this week's victories, challenges, or storms. Proverbs 3:3-5 "Trust in the Lord with all thine heart... He will direct your path."

51 TEACH US TO BE SLOW TO QUARREL

Proverbs 20:3 It is to one's honor to avoid strife, but every fool is quick to quarrel.

Have you ever sat with friends, siblings, cousins, or other family members and discussed something that happened years ago when you were younger? Have you ever been surprised to learn that they recalled the incidents differently than you remembered them? Have you ever been shocked to realize the critical details for them were minor details for you and vice versa? We all see life through our own lens of experience and exposure. We interpret words, body language, and events through our past history. We "connect the dots" using past patterns to gain present understanding.

The first thing we need to understand is that our patterns of life do not necessarily have the same connotation to our coworkers or students. A person can say something to be cute and funny without realizing that the phrase is a significant trigger for anger or hurt in others. Teachers can avoid strife by checking the message before choosing to be angry or offended.

A few people will try to push people's triggers and make others angry or hurt their feelings, but we must not assume that most people are that way. We can avoid a lot of pain and strife in our lives by considering that most people do not purposely go around choosing to attack others with what they say. Even if that is not true of everyone, we will have a better day if we can teach our students and ourselves to be slow to be offended, to assume the best of each person's intent, and to ask the person for clarification of their statement before choosing to be offended.

As we learn to walk in blessing and not cursing, in righteousness and not judgment, we will become slower to judge the words of others and less likely to be offended. The purer our hearts become, the more we are able to overlook offenses from others. Titus 1:15 reads: "To the pure, all things are pure, but to those who are corrupted and do not believe, nothing is pure..."

Dear God, I want to be a person that brings peace and does not stir up strife. Teach me to think the best about others and to be slow to anger. Create in me a clean heart and renew in me a right spirit (Ps. 51:10). Purify my thoughts and heal my past wounds. Give me the wisdom and understanding needed to teach others these truths so that we may all live in greater harmony and tolerance.

52 HUMILITY COMES BEFORE HONOR

I Peter 5:6 *Humble yourselves, therefore, under God's mighty hand, that he may lift you up in due time.*

Even though Mary was the mother of Jesus, there came a time in her life when Jesus became more than her son. She too bowed her knee. Jesus became more than her son; He became her Lord and Savior. Consider for a moment that remarkable transition that Mary experienced.

We all will face transitions in relationships as we age. We often find ourselves following a supervisor or principal younger than us. And sometimes they are much younger and much less experienced than we are. Our challenge is to respect and follow these younger leaders with the goal of helping them to be successful. If we hold on to our rights and our need to be acknowledged for our experience and expertise, the transition will be uncomfortable. But, if we can humble ourselves and remain determined to make the new situation work, God will exalt us in due time. Remember, a man's gift makes way for him.

Trust God to exalt you in his timing. I have had this experience, and I have seen. God bring me alongside my leaders as a helper after I humbly submitted and served my principal. Humble yourself in the sight of God, and He will lift you up.

Dear God, I trust you, and I believe your Word. Fill me with your Grace as I seek to serve the leaders you placed over me. I put my professional career in Your hands.

53 GRANT ME A CHEERFUL HEART

Proverbs 17:22 *A cheerful heart is good medicine but a crushed spirit dries up the bones.* (NIV)

Celebrate this year with joy and appreciation for those on your team. Take time to write notes of gratitude that you have thought about writing but put off until a better time. Everyone needs to be appreciated. They will benefit from being told they are a blessing. Statements or notes of thankfulness can bring cheerfulness that acts as a good medicine for those you serve and those who serve with you. Your greatest gift to those in your small world is to remember them with a note or card.

Failing to say thank you or to compliment a job well done can crush a person's spirit. To serve without appreciation or without acknowledgement of a job well done discourages future effort. We don't compliment for the purpose of manipulation or to get them to continue to serve. Rather, we offer appreciation because it is the right thing to do.

Appreciation and gratitude is also valuable when working with your students. Some of the greatest times with my students was when I took time to acknowledge each student and tell them what I appreciated about them. Sometimes I would point out the talents I saw building in them; other times I spoke of specific acts of kindness I witnessed. This was a wonderful, uplifting way to end a semester or a year.

DEAR GOD: Give us the wisdom to have the courage and time to express our appreciation to our team, our students, and their parents. May our thankfulness become genuine and deeply rooted within us. Help us to realize how many blessings we really have. Give us the willingness to share those blessings with those that bring blessing and richness in our lives.

54 BRING THE CHILDREN TO ME

Mark 10:14 *When Jesus saw this, he was indignant. He said to them, "Let the little children come to me, and do not hinder them, for the kingdom of God belongs to such as these.*

We finished our lunch and were preparing to leave the restaurant when my husband spotted a man with a long white beard with the striking resemblance of Santa Clause. My husband couldn't resist saying something to him. "I have never met you, but I bet I know what you do during the Christmas holidays. You play Santa, right?"

His eyes twinkled and he admitted that he had been Santa in his community for several years. He then asked my husband for his name. He reached in his pocket and pulled out a card and wrote my husband's name on the card and gave it to him. It said, "Dean has been good this year. Santa Clause." He then said "Even big boys and girls stop to speak to me all throughout the year. I take time for all of them." He continued to explain than his portrayal of Santa was for the purpose of explaining the reason for Christmas and

God's love for us all. To him, the Spirit of Christ(mas) was meant to be spread throughout the year, not just in December.

The man's love for people was evident in his walk and his talk. His desire to bring happiness and hope to others influenced his daily life. His willingness to visit with my husband and others that approach him throughout the year showed his compassion and interest in people. We left the restaurant with a smile and a card to remember our encounter with this unique individual.

As I pondered this experience, I realized that we, as Christian teachers, can bring the "Light of the World" to our sphere of influence through everyday encounters in and out of the classroom. We have the opportunity to show the love of Christ and to take time to care about those we serve. We can purpose to build a hope and a future for our students through encouragement, affirmation, and positive input into their lives. We can bring the "Spirit of Christ" to our students and fellow teachers as we exhibit the love of Jesus. WWJD (What Would Jesus Do) would serve us well as we live our lives to serve others.

Dear God, Help me to bring joy and hope into my classroom as I serve my students. Fill my heart with your unconditional love for each child. Give me a vision for their future, and show me specific ways I can be a lasting blessing to those I serve.

55 YOU CAN CHANGE YOUR ATTITUDE

Phil 2:5-8 *Have this mind among yourselves, which is yours in Christ Jesus who, though he was in the form of God, did not count equality with God a thing to be grasped, ⁷but emptied himself, by taking the form of a servant, being born in the likeness of men.*

⁸And being found in human form, he humbled himself by becoming obedient to the point of death, even death on a cross.

As Christians, we can make a difference in our day by choosing the right attitude. When everything seems to be going against us, choosing the right attitude will give us the strength to keep moving forward. We may not be able to control the situation, but one thing we can control is our attitude. It is not what happens to us that affects our lives as much as it is how we respond to what happens to us. When we learn to seek God's perspective about what happens in our lives, we gain the strength to make good choices. The right attitude can change us even when our circumstances don't change.

Two negative attitudes that can destroy our day are "blame" and "self-pity." Blame is an aggressive reaction to an event. It seeks to find a scapegoat and causes us to avoid introspection that would help us learn from our part, if any, in the conflict. On the other hand, self-pity is a passive reaction to a problem. "Woe is me; I don't deserve this; it isn't fair," become our inner thoughts. We begin to feel defenseless and hopeless. Self-pity traps our emotions and blocks our ability to find a way through the offense so we can move forward.

We give away our personal power when we fail to take control of our emotions. We all have control over our responses to our feelings. We can change our thoughts and attitudes much like we flip channels on the television. We must choose to believe the best, hope for the best, and decide to think on good things (Philippians 4:8). We have the power to choose a better action rather than allowing ourselves to simply react to the situation.

How can we apply this in our teaching profession?

Polishing the Apple 2

(1) Apologize when we realize we have offended someone--even if we don't understand why they were offended. Let them know it was not our intent to offend them. Apologize for causing them discomfort (Matthew 15).

(2) Give only a soft answer when being verbally attacked. Let them give their message, before answering back. Then, repeat their message to show we understand before giving any explanation. Apologize if we are even 1% wrong.

(3) Choose to believe that most conflicts are misunderstandings and can be worked out with good communication.

(4) Accept that there will be times when we will not be able to make peace with everyone due to strong differences of opinions or their unwillingness to forgive.

(5) Choose to forgive those who offend us even if they don't ask for forgiveness. Jesus did. It sets us free from the offense. We must not allow ourselves to be prisoners of another person's issue.

Dear God, Give me the courage to act responsibly in times of conflict. Help me to avoid both blame and self-pity. Instead, give me the courage to examine my own heart to look for error, to apologize for even the slightest fault on my part, and insight as I pray for understanding and wisdom to rectify the situation. Lastly, help me to choose humility as I apologize and forgive those involved. I chose to be a peacemaker.

(Thank you, Rev. Rusty Shular of Red Oak, Texas for the sermon that inspired this devotion.)

56 I NEED GOD'S WISDOM FOR THIS SITUATION

Psalm 46:1 *God is our refuge and strength, a very present help in trouble.*

I kept thinking about the difficult situation facing me the next morning. A few months earlier, I attended a seminar on how to deal with students who bully and mock teachers and other students. I knew any authority dealing with this problem could have it blow up in their face if it was not dealt with properly. These students seldom admit to wrong doing and often make the one trying to bring correction look foolish and overbearing. I needed wisdom far beyond any training, experience or intuition I possessed. I needed God's guidance in this situation. After asking God for His help, I fell asleep with the problem on my mind.

I woke up the next morning with the "God idea" of how to counsel the student. When he entered my office, I gave him a Bible; I picked up my Bible. Without referring to the issue at hand, I simply asked him to read a Scripture on mocking. I then asked him to explain what he thought the Scripture meant. He explained it to me and we went to the next Scripture on my list. After we finished reading all of the Scriptures, I asked him if any of these Scriptures had anything to do with him? He bowed his head and began to shed tears of repentance. He not only saw what he had done, but he also admitted that he had been treating students that way for several years. His bullying stopped that day. It was amazing. God knew the key to his heart. It was God's Word that spoke to his need rather than my words. God's way was truly higher than my way.

My answer may not ever be applicable for your situation, but God does have a specific answer for your needs. The answers differ for each conflict, but God is an ever present help in times of trouble. We often fail to receive God's wisdom because we forget to ask God for help. I encourage you to continually depend on God's guidance and wisdom in your daily decisions. Pray about everything. Listen for those "God ideas" only He can bring. God is faithful.

Dear God, It is comforting to me to know that you can give me "God ideas" when I need wisdom. Teach me to humble myself and ask for your wisdom. Build my faith and help me to trust you in every conflict and every confusing decision I face. I want to trust you more.

57 TWO ATTITUDES THAT SUSTAIN US THROUGH TRIALS

James 4:5 *Humble yourselves before the Lord and He will lift you up.*

Humility is key that brings us to a higher plane in the midst of a conflict. Philippians 2:5-8 reports that Jesus emptied himself of pride and position to become a servant to mankind. He obeyed even to the point of dying on the cross. He chose to remain calm when falsely accused. He sought to help others find truth in the midst of his suffering. He trusted God to be his defender.

What is true humility? It is not thinking less of ourselves, but rather it is not thinking of ourselves at all. It is not debasing ourselves, or down playing or denying our strengths. Rather, it is putting our emphasis and attention on others' needs. Jesus placed man's need above his own when he submitted to the crucifixion. If our primary concern is always ourselves, we will never make a difference in others. God wants to make a difference through us. God's love must flow through us to others. Phil 2:3-4 tells us *Do nothing from selfish ambition or conceit, but in humility count others more significant than yourselves.* ⁴ *Let each of you look not only to his own interests, but also to the interests of others.*

The second key attitude that will serve us well in times of conflict is Hope. Bad things happen to good people; things occur that are hard to justify or explain. Also, just as unfair, we see good things happening to bad people. Only as we trust in God can we see beyond our painful experience to discover the gain. Hope believes for the gain. Hope patiently waits for God to bring good out of the bad. We need to hold on to hope believing that better times are coming. The only way we can maintain hope is by maintaining our personal relationship with Jesus Christ. Our hope is tied into God and His promises. Sometimes things happen and it seems nothing good could come from it. But God can bring good out of evil. We must hope in His promises. He can bring good in ways we cannot imagine. (Psalm 61:3)

Let us not be weary in well doing this year. Put your hope in God!

Dear God, Thank you for the strength to walk through conflict in a godly manner. Help me to avoid complaining and arguing. Instead give me the grace to give a soft answer, to apologize when I am wrong, to heal the broken hearted, and to bring glory to your name. Give me the courage to choose to change my attitude. I want to choose to be a servant and a follower of Christ that hopes in God's goodness and grace.

(Thank you, Rev. Rusty Shular of Red Oak for the sermon that inspired this devotion.)

58 COMPASSION IS NOT CONVENIENT!

Luke 10:33-34 *But a Samaritan, as he traveled, came where the man was; and when he saw him, he had compassion on him He went to him and bandaged his wounds, pouring on oil and wine.*

Then he put the man on his donkey, brought him to an inn and took care of him.

The students that fill our classroom are wounded and need our compassion as much as the man who was beaten and robbed. Some of their wounds come from fellow students, and some wounds come from school leaders, neighbors, business people, parents, and other family members. The wounds are deeper than the eyes can see. These wounds are in their hearts and souls.

As teachers, we have the opportunity to be part of the healing process for the hurting students. But let me warn you, it will not be without a price. It will cost you time, emotional energy, prayer time, and interruptions in your schedule. Jesus valued children. He wanted them brought to him. He chose to minister to them individually. He invites us to do the same.

Continual failure is destructive and destroys a student's hope. Success builds hope and gives students the courage to reach for more success. My goal, as a teacher, is to make success possible for my students so they will develop a love for learning and reach for greater knowledge and understanding. The only way I know how to do this for each student is to learn what their strengths, interests and weaknesses are so I can lead them to success. I admit that this takes time, energy, creativity, and sometimes money.

I have read research studies that investigated teacher opinions and struggles with using the differentiated instruction process in the classroom. Although many schools have required teachers to use this method, teachers are finding it difficult and many are just not doing it. I want to encourage you to look at differentiated instruction as a mending process for students that struggle and a gift of challenge for students who are advanced and are otherwise bored.

Let your compassion and prayer lead you as you plan your activities. Look at your students' needs, group them accordingly, and plan your lessons to meet instructional needs. Every lesson may not need to be differentiated if all the students can be successful as a group. But, if there are those that will fail or become disinterested without differentiation, I encourage you to have enough compassion, to meet the needs (emotional as well as academically) of your students.

Help your students discover that learning can be fun and exciting. Ask God to guide you in your planning. You will be surprised how creative you can become with God's help.

Dear God, I want to be compassionate and meet my students' needs. Give me the knowledge, understanding, and creativity needed to differentiate my instruction. Help me to "look beyond my students' faults to see their needs." [You may want to check out the lyrics of the song written by the late Dottie Rambo "He looked beyond my faults, and saw my needs." This song has some awesome lyrics.

59 CHOICES HAVE CONSEQUENCES

Galatians 6:7 *Do not be deceived: God cannot be mocked. A man reaps what he sows (*Galatians 6:7).

We have all studied the scientific principle, "for every action there is a reaction." Every decision or choice has a consequence. Teachers need to train their students in understanding "cause and effect."

"My mom made me late." It is important that our classroom discipline is based on rules with specific consequences to those breaking the rules. The better students understand that they brought the consequences on themselves by disobeying the rule, the sooner the student will choose to follow the rules in the future. If students believe that the teacher had it in for them, or was in a bad mood, or made up the rule, they will not benefit from any consequences they receive. They will put the blame on others. A teacher's consistency and ability to avoid showing favoritism is the only way for students to look inward instead of outward for the cause of the infraction. Students who own their error will more likely avoid the same error in the future.

A teacher that becomes angry at a misbehaving student and reacts negatively is negating a perfect opportunity to teach students self-control and fairness. The teacher is the policeman. The student is the citizen. The rules (laws) are the guidelines. When students fail to follow the rules, they are going against the rule—not the teacher. Therefore, the teacher acts as the servant of the law by enforcing the law. Don't make it personal. Students "earn" the discipline marks or detentions. Teachers do not "give" them. A teacher who understands this principle will be less likely to get angry when discipline is required.

Dear God, Help me to be consistent and fair when dealing with my students. Help me to see my errors when I get emotionally involved in a discipline issue. I want my discipline to be for my student's benefit, not mine.

60 DISCIPLINE REQUIRES ACTION, NOT JUST WORDS

Proverbs 29:19 *A servant will not be corrected by words: for though he understand he will not answer.*

Do you ever find yourself reminding students over and over again what they should do or not do? Do you find yourself dealing with the same misbehavior day after day? Do you give warnings or threats? Do you find yourself resenting students for not doing as you ask? Do you raise the tone of your voice in frustration when dealing with certain students? If so, you may need to reevaluate your approach to discipline. Today's scripture reminds us that students will not be corrected by words alone; they require consequences.

Discipline is not a bad or negative thing. The discipline policy is for the students and not just for the teacher. Students learn best in a well-managed environment. Classroom rules build a sense of security and are foundational to effective teaching. Students care who is in charge. In fact, certain students will test the boundaries (rules) to see if they really exist. When the rules are only partially followed or sporadically enforced, students consider them to be suggestions rather than rules. A teacher who applies discipline irregularly will build resentment. When a student is given a mark for the same behavior that was ignored over and over again in the past, the entire class will resent the disciplinary action. Students know what the written rules contain, but, to the students, they are only "real rules" if the teacher enforces them consistently.

Reminders are appropriate for the first three or four days of school, but, after that, you begin the trap of "warnings." Warnings are a sign that you are not being consistent and/or you are not in control. Consistent discipline creates a community of cooperation and a sense of security. A productive classroom is a well-managed, consistently disciplined classroom.

Discipline is not necessarily negative. Discipline can mean learning to follow a regiment, practicing procedures, and producing results through participation and cooperation. Also, a well-disciplined classroom is not necessarily quiet; it can be active and verbal as long as students are following the teacher's guidelines for the activity.

If you have blown your discipline policy, "you can begin again". (Read devotion #62.) Students want and need discipline

Dear God, Sometimes I struggle with consistency in discipline. Give me wisdom and understanding as I work to instruct and lead my students toward a better managed classroom. Give me the courage to begin again in the middle of the school year.

61 LET PRAYER BE A NORMAL EXPERIENCE IN MY LIFE

Romans 12:12 *Be joyful in hope, patient in affliction, faithful in prayer.*

As I listen to the news and hear of the tornadoes, flooding, and blizzards happening throughout the United States, I find myself continually whispering a prayer for God's grace and mercy for those in the paths of these storms. My heart feels for those experiencing trauma, but I know there is hope in knowing God is with each one. I then turn my heart toward joy as I remind myself how God can take tragedy and turn it into blessing.

I once had a woman tell me of the time her house caught fire and she lost everything. It was a devastating experience. She then began to tell of the kindness of friends, neighbors and even people she had never met. She showed me several pairs of shoes that people provided for her. They were expensive shoes that she had never been able to afford. She continued to explain how God provided for all of her family's needs. In a strange way, her greatest tragedy taught her a deeper reliance on God and his provisions.

No matter what trials or afflictions you face this week, God is aware of your needs. He is a comforter when you are troubled, a provider when you have needs, a friend when you feel lonely, a protector when you are in danger or threatened, and a defender when you are falsely accused. He invites you to come to him and He will give you rest.

Too often we forget the last part of this week's verse--"Be faithful in prayer." We must faithfully pray about every concern and need that God lays on our hearts. We can then praise him abundantly and thank Him for the answers as we see His hand move on our behalf. If we fail to make our requests known, we lose the blessing of seeing the hand of God move on our behalf. Every answered prayer in my life has built a stronger and lasting trust in God and his willingness to hear and answer my prayers. Make prayer a daily part of your lives. Learn to pray as you go. Pray as you sit, as you walk, as you work, and as you lie down.

Lastly, as teachers, pray for the needs of your students. It is exciting to see God at work. Pray for their families, for their friendships, and for their educational needs. God is active in your classrooms. Invite him to be a daily part of your planning and teaching. It always makes a difference when I pray.

Dear God, I invite you to be involved in every part of my life. Continue to direct me and teach me how to pray about the things that matter to me. I love to watch as you make yourself known to me through answered prayer.

62 YOU CAN BEGIN AGAIN

Lamentations 3:22-23-- *Because of the LORD's great love we are not consumed, for his compassions never fail. They are new every morning; great is your faithfulness.*

Don't you just love to begin a new semester or a new school year. Summer and Christmas breaks provide time to re-group and adjust our plans to meet yearly goals. However, anytime is a good time for re-vamping our discipline plan. If you have had some difficult discipline experiences, hopefully, the following will encourage you to press forward to success.

Some students seem to need to test boundaries. They only respond to rules that are consistently applied. A rule that is occasionally enforced, but ignored at other times is no longer a rule. It simply becomes a suggestion. Students will often believe that suggestions should not have consequences. A teacher giving discipline for a poorly enforced rule will likely be accused of unfair discipline practices The student receiving the discipline will feel picked on and singled out and become angry and resentful. Their offense will be shared with other classmates and you may have several students angry with you for enforcing a rule.

For rules to be an effective management tool, students must realize that your rules are firm and there is no value in testing them over and over again. Consistency offers security to students.

Do you ever find yourself reminding your students that they are not suppose to (rule); Do you tell them that it is against the rules? Do you find yourself giving students warnings and telling the students multiple times to stop breaking the rule? Please consider that each time you warn students you are giving them one more chance to disobey the rule. Perhaps you are inadvertently training students how often they can disobey before there are consequences. Perhaps they are learning how much you can tolerate before you apply the rule. Ever had students obey just before you get ready to throw "the book" at them?

I was guilty of this classroom fiasco multiple times before I found a way out of the cycle. To correct my mistakes, I first brought out the rule book and had a meeting with my students. I asked my students to forgive me for not following the rules. I explained that it was my responsibility to follow the rules as much as it was their responsibility to follow the rules. Then I explained that beginning now, I planned to enforce the rules as they are written—no warnings or reminders. It was my way of getting a new start. I reviewed every rule and asked if anyone had questions. AND, THEN I began to follow the rules. It was amazing. The students knew the rules. The testing of the rules became less and less and the classroom became calm and education resumed. I soon realized that I was as much the problem as my students. My students wanted structure and guidelines. They wanted me to keep the classroom orderly so they could learn. I soon understood that they needed me to be consistent. I learned that rules are important to students too. Thankfully, as I gained experience, I had to begin again less and less each year.

Dear God, Give me the courage to revamp my approach to discipline. I need wisdom and guidance in how to approach my students with humility and leadership. Thank you for promising to give me abundant wisdom as I seek you in this particularly awkward time of the year. I choose to follow the rules and lead my students to better self-discipline.

63 WASH AWAY THE "YUCK" OF THE DAY

Psalm 1:1-2 *Blessed is the one who does not walk in step with the wicked or stand in the way that sinners take or sit in the company of mockers, but whose delight is in the law of the* LORD, *and who meditates on his law day and night.*

Robert Robinson wrote the 1737 hymn entitled *Come Thou Fount of Every Blessing* that included the words "Prone to wander, Lord I feel it, Prone to leave the God I love."

The Bible describes the followers of Jesus as sheep that need a shepherd. Sheep are prone to wander. Christian teachers need protection from deception and wrong influences. Constant exposure to wrong thoughts and unscriptural philosophies can affect our perspectives and decisions no matter how long we have followed Christ.

Psalm 1 instructs us to watch where we walk, stand and sit. This does not just refer to the company we keep, but also to the influences we allow to speak into our lives. We must be careful to fill our hearts with the "living water" from God's Word so we can be a blessing to our students. Strength and renewal come when we "delight" in God's laws and when we "meditate" on them continually.

As teachers, we must learn to allow God's living water to wash away the "yuck" of the day. We need God to erase the "stinking thinking" that leads us to defeat. These daily attitude adjustments enable us to have something of value to pour out to our students.

We are not to feel condemned, but rather to realize that we are prone to wander and forget. Perhaps this would be a good day to recommit to daily Bible reading and prayer. Remember, no condemnation. We are all prone to wander.

Dear God, I want to follow you closer, to understand your ways more, and to be the teacher you want me to be. Thank you for helping me to get back on track. Great is your faithfulness.

64 TEACHERS CAN BE BULLIES TOO

Ephesians 4:29, 32 (KJV) *Let no corrupt communication proceed out of your mouth, but that which is good to the use of edifying, that it may minister grace unto the hearers. ...32 And be ye kind one to another, tenderhearted, forgiving one another...*

According to www.stopbullying.gov, *Bullying is unwanted, aggressive behavior ... that involves a real or perceived power imbalance. The behavior is repeated, or has the potential to be repeated, over time. Bullying includes actions such as making threats, spreading rumors, attacking someone physically or verbally, and excluding someone from a group on purpose.*

When I was in high school, I joined Future Teachers of America (FTA) and was allowed to spend one day a month in a teacher's classroom at a local school. I was helping out in a third grade classroom when I observed a situation that I considered bullying from the teacher. The teacher had a spelling contest in progress that included a class reward if everyone in the class made no less than 90% on their spelling test. After the tests were graded, the teacher called a young boy to her desk and began to fuss at him in front of the class for not passing the test. She told him that she wished he had never moved to their town. She continued to say that he always messed up their contests and made everything worse for the class. Tears filled the boys eyes as he slumped his shoulders and returned to his seat. I assumed her goal was to shame him into doing better in his spelling tests. In my opinion, she bullied him.

Several times I have observed teachers who felt the need to motivate students by shaming them. A negative attack usually reaps a negative response. Students are not motivated by threats, put downs, or intimidation. They may cower to the teacher's authority outside, but inside they are building a wall of resentment each time the teacher is unkind or attacking.

Ephesians 4 calls all of us to be careful with our words. We are instructed to be kind, tenderhearted, and forgiving toward our students. Our words are to be words of life that edify and build students up. These words are to encourage students to try harder and to believe that they can do better.

When you find yourself at your wits end with a student, it is better to excuse yourself for a minute or two to get yourself together, or to postpone consequences for the offense until you can deal with the situation in such a way that benefits the student. All discipline and correction should be for the student's benefit. It should never be for retribution.

Check your past behavior to see if you have any bullying behavior in the way you deal with your students. Let God change your heart and give you tenderness toward each of your students. Refuse to play the part of the "teacher bully".

Dear God, Search me and know if there is any wicked way in me. Help me to be kind and tenderhearted to each one of my students. Forgive me for the times I handled things wrong, and help me to build the ability to respond like you in every situation that arises in my classroom.

65 WELCOME PARENT CONFERENCES

James 1:19 ... *be quick to listen, slow to speak and slow to become angry. James 3:2 We all stumble in many ways. Anyone who is never at fault in what they say is perfect, able to keep their whole body in check.*

At the beginning of my teaching career, I dreaded when parents called the office and requested a conference with me. The meetings with parents were often instigated by trouble, complaints, or frustrations. However, I eventually came to understand that these meetings could be productive, insightful, and useful in helping me work with specific students. No matter how much I dreaded an unpleasant confrontation, I determined to try my best to use it as a stepping stone toward building a parent/teacher team.

First, assume there is a misunderstanding or miscommunication at the base of every complaint. Students often carry home incomplete messages to their parents. This will help you deal with confrontation more calmly. Begin by welcoming the parents and offering them something to drink if you have it available. Let them know you are glad they came.

Next, invite the parents to explain their need for a conference. Listen without interruption or explanation. Make a note of things you need to address. Ask questions for clarification, but don't defend yourself until they have had their say. People cannot listen to what you have to say until they first feel that you received their message. In fact, parents will repeat themselves again and again, until they feel you understand the reasons they came to the meeting. No matter how emotional or loud the parents may be, your quiet, listening, and caring demeanor will help them to gain more control. It is important to summarize their message before you continue to explain yourself. You want to make sure you heard them right, and they know that you understand their message.

Don't just act like you are listening. Really listen. Your goal is to understand your student better so you can be more successful in your educational efforts. Calmly explain your perspective of the issue including any school policies you are required to follow. Be gentle in your explanation. Try to empathize with the parent. Don't worry about who is right or wrong or who wins--look for solutions to the problem. Allow the parent to offer suggestions on how the issue can be rectified. Be quick to apologize for any oversight or unthoughtful thing you might have done. Apologize even if you did not intend to be thoughtless. Apologize for their offense even if you didn't feel what you did should have caused offense. You are trying to rectify the situation. Choose to be a peacemaker. Try to understand the parent's or student's perspective and why they took offense.

If possible, come into agreement with the parents to be a co-worker with them in educating their child. The parents have years of experience with their child compared to your few months. Glean from their experiences in past school years. Try to understand the pressures at home. Seek a solution that will work for you and the parent. Present yourself as an advocate for the child. Let the parent know you want to work with them and their child to help them succeed.

Lastly, when the conference is over, be discrete about the things discussed in the conference. Too often teachers share their frustrations in the teachers' lounge afterwards. I encourage you to only speak words that edify and build up in the lounge. You can bring feelings of defeat and anger to others if you speak negatively about leaders, parents, teachers or students.

Dear God, Help me to willingly listen and respond to parents. Give me wisdom to hear their concerns and the creativity to find solutions that work for parents, students, and teachers. Give us the courage to build a team that can live together and work toward common goals.

66 USE CURRENT EVENTS TO TEACH CHARACTER?

Deuteronomy 11:19 *Teach them to your children, talking about them when you sit at home and when you walk along the road, when you lie down and when you get up.*

In verse two of this chapter Moses wrote "...your children were not the ones who saw and experienced the discipline of the Lord your God..." Moses is pleading with the Israelites to pass on their experiences, knowledge and wisdom gained as they traveled through the wilderness. The people saw awesome miracles, felt multiple emotions of success and failure, watched as some reaped the outcome of their wrong decisions, and saw many reap the benefits of doing what was right. Moses pled with the parents to pass these experiences on to their children for their preservation! It was not for enjoyment, or historical knowledge; it was for their future success as a people.

Gaining a full perspective of world events of the past can help students interpret what is currently happening in their world. Teachers need to take time to allow students to ask questions and gain knowledge regarding current events. Of course, the age of the student determines the depth and amount of discussion that can be allowed. High school and even junior high students would benefit from discussions of current issues that may be bothering them.

Recently, I was visiting with a student when he made the statement that all police were bad. I took the opportunity to share with him the need to avoid prejudices toward any group of people. I told him the correct statement would be "Some police officers are bad, but some are not bad." This discussion led into the topic of respect for authority. I told him that we respect police officers because of their position, not because of who they are as a person. We discussed the need for law and for law enforcement. We also discussed the correct response to a police officer should he ever be pulled over. This was truly a teachable moment!

When possible, I would encourage you to take time to address students' questions about real life situations. You don't have to have all the answers. You don't have to spend a lot of time on the subject. Without being authoritative or giving ultimatums, you can listen to their perspective and share any insight you may have gained in your life experiences. Ask God to help you recognize teachable moments, and to give you the wisdom in what and/or what not to share.

Dear God, Give me the courage and the wisdom to address current events with my students when they ask for understanding. First, help me to identify any prejudices in my own life so I can deal with them. Then, give me the guidance to gently lead my students into your truth.

67 SUCCESSFUL LEADERS MUST BE MATURE

Philippians 3:13-15 ... I do not consider myself yet to have taken hold of it. But one thing I do: Forgetting what is behind and straining toward what is ahead, ¹⁴ I press on toward the goal to win the prize for which God has called me heavenward in Christ Jesus.¹⁵ All of us, then, who are mature should take such a view of things.

I look back at the early years of my teaching career and shudder at some of the stern, thoughtless things I said and did as a teacher. Unfortunately, experience and maturity are mostly acquired with time and maturity. Although every teacher has to walk through the process of maturing, we can gain a more mature perspective by understanding the things Jesus taught about relationships with our fellowman.

Some valuable instructions from the Bible that I have been central to my development as an educator are listed below:

1. Matthew 5:41 Be willing to go the extra mile with your students. Give them the help and support they need even if you have to give up some of your personal time.
2. Matthew 6:14 Forgive everyone; let it go. Pray for the strength to forgive even the worst offenses.
3. Matthew 7:1-2 Because God offers us mercy and grace, we ought to do the same for our students and co-workers. Do not condemn or judge. Students are diamonds in the rough.
4. Galatians 5:22-23 Don't lose your temper; practice self-control. Anger gives the signal that you are out-of-control. God can give you the strength to let go of you anger.
5. Luke 9:23 Deny yourself, take up the cross and follow Christ. Give up your rights and pick up your responsibilities. Seek to serve rather than to be served.
6. Leviticus 9:18 Don't hold grudges. Release your students, parents, and co-workers when they offend you. Choose to love your students and co-workers regardless of their behavior.
7. Matthew 5:7 God desires us to deal with each other in mercy and love. Examine your heart before you respond to conflict. Be quick to listen and slow to speak. Choose your battles. Some victories are not worth the damage left after the conflict.

Personal maturity will be one of your most valuable assets. Make it a priority in your life to develop Christian character.

Dear God, Guide me into your truth. Give me the courage and wisdom to listen to your instructions on how to treat other people. Give me a teachable heart.

68 DOES YOUR GRADING PEN HAVE A HEART?

Zechariah 7:9 *Administer true justice; show mercy and compassion to one another*

Have you ever failed to read instructions while filling out a medical or business form and wrote the wrong information in the blanks provided? Have you ever had to download or ask for a clean copy because you messed up a whole section? I have done that more than once. The doctor's receptionist simply smiled, said, "No problem," and let me begin again. She didn't scold me or charge me an extra fee for needing a second try.

Unfortunately, many teachers are not so gracious with their students. Entire sections of questions are commonly marked with a red "X" when it is obvious that the student misunderstood what to do and/or did not read the directions. You may be saying, "But students need to learn to read the instructions and pay closer attention." That is true, but it doesn't take the receptionist at the doctor's office to scold me for me to realize my error. Having to redo the section automatically reminds me.

Grades are a measurement of progress. They should not be used to punish a student for immaturity or irresponsibility. When questions are mismarked, the only way to get an accurate measurement of the student's knowledge is to have them redo that section of the assignment or test. Otherwise, your grade is measuring a bad day, a lapse in attention, or immaturity. None of these should be reflected in your gradebook.

Recently I went to a new doctor and had to complete forms for the files. I dutifully completed each blank. I returned it to the receptionist only to have her call me back up to the window. "Could you put your name on the form and sign it, please?" Yes, you got it! How many times have teachers reminded students to put their name on their papers? Again, taking off points is not a correct use of the grading pen for forgetting your name. Gentle reminders work best. I made it a habit to remind the class to put their name on their paper/test just before they began their work. This seemed to help.

Check the heartbeat of your grading pen. If it is lacking the flow of compassion and gentleness, consider giving it an overhaul. It will be a positive change to your teaching experience.

Dear God, Help me to discern what is just and unjust in my grading practices. I want to please you in all that I do.

69 LET EVERY WORD BE ACCEPTABLE

Proverbs 10:32 *The lips of the righteous know what is fitting, but the mouth of the wicked only what is perverse*

Every word that comes from our lips reveals the condition of our hearts. What is pure within will be proven pure in conversation, and what is perverted within will be revealed as impure during constant interactions in the school setting.

During the school year, unknowingly, we may reveal our true motives and heart-throbs. After spending weeks and weeks together, the "Real you' will probably peek through our facade. Teachers cannot escape the scrutinizing eyes of parents, students, and staff. People will detect our weaknesses. Our "fleshly nature" is often exposed in times of conflict. We need to prepare ourselves to guard our tongues, watch our actions, and apologize when we blow it. We are not God! We will make mistakes. We need to accept this about ourselves. BE REAL! BE HUMAN! We have limitations, and God is still growing us toward becoming more like Him.

However, we can't use this as an excuse to "act out". Leaders are judged with a higher judgment than the average person is judged (teachers specifically). Parents and students will expect a higher standard of behavior from us. After all, teachers are models set before the students--silently inviting, "Come follow me. I will show you the way." We must strive to be the leader we would want our own kids to follow. Avoid suggestive statements, belittling remarks, questionable jokes, or negative facial expressions. These have no place in a Christian teacher's daily walk. The damage done from such responses can be far reaching. An ill chosen statement, an act of disobedience toward our supervisor, an unacceptable joke, or an unrighteous response can destroy a student's trust for leaders, not only for us, as the current teacher, but also for other leaders in years to come. As we seek to be an imitator of Christ, we will become leaders worth following.

Spend time with God each morning before you leave your home. Prepare your heart for the day. Hear God's heartbeat for your situation and for the needs of your students. Put on your armor--salvation, righteousness, faith, truth and the gospel of peace--daily. Learn to listen carefully and answer after you have considered your words. We cannot depend upon yesterday's success to bring us success today.

Dear God: *Search me, oh God, and know my heart today... see if there be some wicked way in me* (Psalm 139:23-24). Cleanse me from unrighteousness. *Let the words of my mouth and the meditations of my heart be acceptable* (Psalm 19:14) today and this year.

70 THERE IS POWER IN GENTLENESS

Colossians 3:12 *Therefore, as God's chosen people, holy and dearly loved, clothe yourselves with compassion, kindness, humility, gentleness and patience.*

We often think of gentle people as being timid, easy going, perhaps without strong opinions, and basically weak in decision making. All of these assumptions are inaccurate. It takes great strength of character and self-control to be able to "clothe yourselves with compassion, kindness, humility, gentleness, and patience." The verb "clothe" infers the need to make purposeful changes to your natural responses. We are being called to choose a different response from our automatic reactions. A gentle leader must practice mature responses when they face challenges. They must prepare themselves spiritually and mentally for battles that may arise throughout the day.

The Bible tells us to be quick to listen and slow to speak. Delaying our response to conflict may save us a lot of regret. The tongue is a powerful tool. Proverbs 15:1 reminds us that "A gentle answer turns away wrath, but a harsh word stirs up anger." Proverbs 18:21 tells us that "the tongue has the power of life and death..."

Determine to practice gentleness when dealing with co-workers and students this week. It will serve you well. I Peter 3:4 tells us "the unfading beauty of a gentle and quiet spirit is of great worth in God's sight."

Dear God, Teach me to deal with my students and my fellow teachers with gentleness and concern. I want to reflect your kindness and gentleness in all I do this week.

71 PERSEVERANCE IS THE KEY TO SUCCESS

2 Corinthians 16-18 *Therefore we do not lose heart. Though outwardly we are wasting away, yet inwardly we are being renewed day by day. For our light and momentary troubles are achieving for us an eternal glory that far outweighs them all. So we fix our eyes not on what is seen, but on what is unseen, since what is seen is temporary, but what is unseen is eternal.*

Most teachers chose the field of education because they wanted to make a difference; they wanted to help students become productive citizens and successful family members. Teachers seldom see the full outcome of their training. The full benefit of the training will be realized years later when our students have moved on to higher grades. Giving without being able to see the full results can cause us to lose heart and wonder if we ever made a difference in our students.

Scripture tells us to keep pressing forward. Keep pursuing the best for our students. We must not let our "momentary troubles" become our focus and blur the end prize. We must see our students as incomplete paintings--canvases in progress. Some dark shadows may momentarily seem to destroy the picture and make everything seem lost. But, with God, all things are possible. He can make things beautiful with time. We must never give up on God's ability to use the seeds of love, compassion, and truth we plant to, in His time, grow a useful and wonderful young man or woman.

Refuse to magnify a child's negative traits. Remember, every negative trait is a positive trait misused. Satan loves to take our strengths and twist them for harm instead of good. Our job is to ask God to help us recognize the strengths of our students and seek understanding of how to help the child use that talent for good instead of harm. Just as a farmer must wait for the harvest after he plants, teachers must also plant with perseverance and endure the daily classroom frustrations. We must gain a larger perspective than this day, or this term, or even this year. Keep planting, keep teaching, keep caring, and keep trying your best. Your rewards are eternal. God is faithful.

Dear God, Forgive me for the times I get discouraged with teaching. Help me not to lose faith in what you have called me to do. I know that you will watch over the seeds that I plant and bring a harvest in due time.

72 LEAD ME WITH YOUR VOICE

John 16:13-16 *But when he, the Spirit of truth, comes, he will guide you into all truth. He will not speak on his own; he will speak only what he hears, and he will tell you what is yet to come. *[14]*He will bring glory to me by taking from what is mine and making it known to you. *[15]*All that belongs to the Father is mine. That is why I said the Spirit will take from what is mine and make it known to you.*

I had a very unusual experience, but one that left a lasting impression upon my life. As I was driving to school, the thought came to me "You're going to speak in chapel today." I taught at a large Christian school. Pastors or guest speakers spoke in the weekly chapels—not teachers. I quietly laughed to myself and thought, "What an egotistical, unrealistic thought." I dismissed the thought and drove on to work. My principal was waiting for me when I entered the school building. "Mrs. Wyrick," he said. "I think you should do chapel today. Will you?"

I agreed to speak and quickly found a quiet place to be alone with God. I first asked for forgiveness for my unbelief and lack of listening. I realized that God wanted to give me instructions as I drove to school, but I failed to recognize his "still small voice." I asked for guidance and my instructions came quickly. I spoke before 350 students within 30 minutes.

God can direct your day. The Spirit of God that dwells in each of His children will guide you, if you have a heart that listens. He can give you creativity and supernatural wisdom. He can lead you with specific guidance. I challenge each teacher to seek the face of God until His voice and His direction becomes clear to you and He begins to direct your path.

Dear God, Forgive me for the times that I failed to recognize your voice from my own thoughts. Also, forgive me for those times that I went my own direction because it made more sense at the time. Lead me into your present truth for today.

73 LOVE THE CHILD; CORRECT THE BEHAVIOR

Proverbs 3:11-12 *My son, do not despise the LORD's discipline and do not resent his rebuke, [12] because the LORD disciplines those he loves, as a father the son he delights in.*

Solomon gives us the key to loving correction. Psalm 139:16 tells us that "All the days ordained for me were written in your book before one of them came to be." Our Heavenly Father knows the potential we have built into our being. He knows what we can be, and He lovingly and unceasingly leads us toward the path that we should go. When we rebel and choose an alternate route, he corrects us. Not because he hates us, but because he knows what we will miss if we get off track.

Teachers can also look beyond the present to see the potential that God has placed into each child. If you truly love your students, you will gently but firmly insist on certain behavioral changes when students act out. As you train and discipline students, keep your eyes on their future, not their present. Students are not always loveable in their present situation. Because of this, we must be able to see past the current behavior to truly love them through correction into a better path.

God offers you the grace to love the unlovely child. He said, "My grace is sufficient for you, . . ." Cor. 12:9) "If any of you lacks wisdom, he should ask God,..." (James 1:5) Allow God to do the work in your heart—a work of unconditional love. It is a work of the Holy Spirit, not just a decision. Pray over your attitudes. Pray for wisdom and supernatural love for that problematic student. Pray for wisdom to understand how to approach the child in a way that they can receive correction and eventually be grateful for your instruction. Remain in the presence of God long enough to be filled with His love for the difficult student.

Dear God, It's hard to love students who give me trouble. I want to love the way you love. I want to walk in unconditional love, but it will have to be your Spirit that does that in me. I submit myself to you. Work in me what I cannot do in myself.

74 WATCH OVER THE SEED THAT I PLANTED

1 Corinthians 3:5-8 *What, after all, is Apollos? And what is Paul? Only servants, through whom you came to believe--as the Lord has assigned to each his task. ⁶ I planted the seed, Apollos watered it, but God made it grow. ⁷ So neither he who plants nor he who waters is anything, but only God, who makes things grow. ⁸ The man who plants and the man who waters have one purpose, and each will be rewarded according to his own labor.*

The year is quickly passing. I have tried to be faithful to plant good seed in each of my students. But, in all honesty, I haven't seen very many changes in their lives. Well, maybe in a few students, but I wanted to see more. I wanted to make a difference. Nevertheless, some students never quite discovered the "light." Please, dear Heavenly Father, watch over the seeds I planted.

One of the most difficult things about teaching is the lack of closure in so many areas. We plant; we water; we plant, and we water day after day, week after week. And, sometimes the new growth doesn't pop out of the soil no matter how we coax or counsel the student. Some things take more time than others; some students mature slower, and other students harden their hearts and refuse to grow.

Because there are so many factors involved in growth, we must understand the Scripture listed above to keep our chins up and our hearts focused on the task at hand. Teachers are generally seed planters; however, there are times that we water where other teachers have planted. And, there are times when we see the plant sprout and even bloom. But we will seldom see the ripened fruit since this stage usually develops later into adulthood. Oh yes, a few do come back to thank us and let us know how significant we were to their lives, but not very many.

Therefore, our satisfaction comes from knowing that we were faithful to plant and to water where we were assigned. Our rewards are eternal. Someday we will understand the importance of every seed, of every kindness, and every "extra mile" given to the student with extra needs. But, for now, we must remain faithful to plant daily and commit each seed to the Father's loving care. We must never forget that it was only "God (that) made it grow"(1 Cor. 3:6b).

Dear God, Help me to be faithful to my calling of planting or watering. I want to use every opportunity I can to plant your truth and your love into the hearts of my students. Give me wise words of counsel as I water your planted truth by making your word practical to current situations. Direct my day and help me to see your plan for today's planting assignments.

Or END OF YEAR PRAYER

Dear God, Thank you for helping me through this year. Bring growth to the good seeds I planted, and cause any destructive or negative seed I inadvertently planted to be swept away without bearing bad fruit. I want to be a faithful servant. I place my words and my deeds of this year at your feet. I trust you enough to release this year's struggles and successes into your hands. Continue to give me wisdom and strength as I enter into the summer season. I want to trust you in all my ways.

75 BEAUTY OUT OF ASHES

Isaiah 61:3 ...*provide for those who grieve in Zion—to bestow on them a crown of beauty instead of ashes, the oil of joy instead of mourning, and a garment of praise instead of a spirit of despair. They will be called oaks of righteousness, a planting of the Lord for the display of his splendor.*

I believe that God's timing is perfect. I used to fret about things that "needed" to be done and I couldn't seem to find the time or resources to get it accomplished. As I mature, my faith in God is becoming deeper and simpler. He walks with me. He knows my needs before I ever voice them. He is my hiding place when things go wrong. He is the glory and lifter of my head. He is my strength, my shield, my wisdom, and my peace. I'm seeking to learn how to walk like a little child--not fretting about what is not or what might or might not be. I want to rely on my Heavenly Father who leads me down the path of life. I am learning to trust in His wisdom and His direction. I desire to daily humble myself before God and learn to accept His plan even when I don't understand why or where it is leading. As long as He is with me, I will be okay--He is my hope for now and for eternity.

I have come to believe that God is more interested in relationship (friendship and communion) with us than He is with what we can "DO" for Him. I believe He wants to plant His truths so deep into our beings that when the "ship falls prey to unexpected storms", we will come through undamaged--maybe roughed up but not destroyed.

I also believe that because we live in a "fallen planet" with imperfect people, people get hurt just because we are here on earth—not because God is punishing us or wanting to teach us a lesson, but because natural laws bring natural consequences. Nevertheless, God has promised to bring "beauty out of our ashes"--in His time when we humble ourselves before His greatness and allow Him to lead us down the path He chooses.

Dear God, Thank you for your unending patience that leads us to a greater knowledge of you. Help my heart to remain pliable and teachable as I walk down the path of life. Truly, your goal for me is to learn to trust and obey you in all things.

CR: Restoration

76 HAVE WE LEARNED "AT ONCE" OBEDIENCE?

Matthew 4:18-20 *As Jesus was walking beside the Sea of Galilee, he saw two brothers, Simon called Peter and his brother Andrew. They were casting a net into the lake, for they were fishermen.* [19]

"Come, follow me," Jesus said, "and I will make you fishers of men." [20] At once they left their nets and followed him.

Two brothers, busy doing their daily labor, received an invitation that would forever change their lives. Have you ever wondered what prompted these two men to forsake everything they owned to follow Christ? They never questioned where they were going, or how long they would be gone. They simply dropped their nets and followed him. Surely they sensed a supernatural drawing toward Jesus like the two men who walked on the road to Emmaus who said in Luke 24:32 *...Were not our hearts burning within us while he talked with us on the road and opened the Scriptures to us?*

Do you require lengthy explanations and persuasive speeches before you are willing to obey a directive given by your leader? Are you a "blessing" to your administrator or a "challenge?" These questions are important issues to ponder. If we, as teachers, have not learned to obey willingly and instantly, how can we train our students in obedience? Who we are speaks louder than anything we say.

Obedience is a heart issue, not just an action. You may recall the story of the little boy who told his mother, "I may be sitting down on the outside, but I'm standing up on the inside." His obedience was only on the surface. Compliance is not necessarily obedience.

Isaiah 1:9 speaks of being "willing and obedient" which results in receiving the "best of the land." When we learn complete obedience from the heart--not blind obedience, but rather the ability to choose to follow because it is right--we will experience greater satisfaction and success throughout our life. Good followers make great leaders.

Dear God, Change my heart. Give me a willing spirit to follow the leader(s) you placed over me. Teach me to be obedient—inside and out—so that I might "eat the good of the land."

77 STINKING THINKING BRINGS DESTRUCTION

Proverbs 23:7 *For as he thinketh in his heart, so is he...* (KJV)

Some people have their own personal rain cloud that they carry with them all day, and other people are rays of sunshine when they walk into the classroom. Your attitude can make all the difference in your success as a teacher. The one thing we <u>can</u> control is our attitude.

When everything seems to be going against us, attitude is that one thing that helps us to keep moving forward. It is not what happens to us as much as it is how we respond to what happens to us. Discovering the positive when something happens in our lives can help us move forward. Our attitude can change us even if our circumstances do not change.

Two self-defeating, stinking-thinking attitudes we must avoid to keep our actions in check are blame and self-pity. Sometimes it is our fault and sometimes it is the other person's fault, but blame does not solve an issue. Most people do not set out to hurt the other person. Bad things just happen sometimes. Be quick to forgive no matter who is at fault. Choosing self-pity in the situation is self-defeating and non-productive. The only way to turn a bad situation in to a positive experience is to learn from it. This requires complete honesty and a commitment to forgive and move forward.

Practice being happy. Refuse to allow your mind to dwell on negative things. Avoid negative people who bring you down. If possible, avoid adverse reports about others. Learn to think about good things and reject the personal rain cloud that so easily attaches to our day. Choose sunshine, and your students will enjoy you as a teacher.

Dear God, I have been guilty of stinking thinking. Help me to recognize that trap and give me the courage to turn away from negative thoughts and dwell on positive things. I want to be the ray of sunshine in my classroom.

78 FORGIVE AND RESTORE YOUR STUDENTS

II Samuel 9:8, 11 *Mephibosheth bowed down and said, "What is your servant, that you should notice a dead dog like me?" ...So Mephibosheth ate at David's table like one of the king's sons.*

Mephibosheth was King Saul's grandson (Jonathan's son). When Saul's kingdom collapsed, a servant hid Mephibosheth to protect him from his grandfather's enemies. Several years later, Mephibosheth was discovered and brought to King David. Mephibosheth feared for his life because he was King Saul's grandson. He told David that he was a dead dog--"dead" because he was a useless cripple and unable to be a threat to David's kingdom; "dog" because he was bowing to the lowest position possible to plead for his life. What Mephibosheth did not know was that David wanted to exalt and honor Mephibosheth because of King David's close friendship with his father, Jonathan. David esteemed Mephibosheth and gave him a place in the palace and treated him like a king's son.

This famous Bible story reminds us of God's eternal work of salvation for each of us. We come before God with all of our impurities and past baggage deserving of death. He not only pardons us from our past, but He exalts us to the position of a King's son. May the truth of what Jesus did at the cross sink deep into our hearts. Jesus died on the cross and offered "undeserved" forgiveness to us while we were YET in our sin.

As we allow this truth of "undeserved forgiveness" to become a reality in our lives, we will be equipped to forgive our students for their offenses even before they repent. "Blessed are the merciful, for they shall receive mercy" (Matthew 5:7). David not only pardoned Mephibosheth; he also RESTORED him to his position in the King's palace. When offenses occur in your classroom--correct, forgive, and then restore the student. Be Christ's hand extended. Be an example of God's love and grace. After the correction is complete, welcome your wayward student back into the routine of your classroom.

Dear God, Let this truth be part of my daily life and a truth planted in my heart. I thank you for your forgiveness toward me. Teach me to forgive and to restore my students

79 RENEW YOUR STRENGTH

Isaiah 40:31 *But they that wait upon the LORD shall renew their strength; they shall mount up with wings as eagles; they shall run, and not be weary; and they shall walk, and not faint.* (KJV)

How "alive" are you spiritually today? Have you fallen into the trap of being too busy for your personal devotions? Has your personal and school duties pushed aside your quiet times with God? If so, I urge you to find the "Secret Place" with God again. Your ministry will be affected when you find your spiritual fervor dwindle.

To win students to Christ, a teacher must have a vibrant, close and personal relationship with God. Your excitement and interest about the things of God will be a light in a dark world. Your students will only be drawn to Christ through your consistent lifestyle of love, joy, peace, longsuffering, gentleness, goodness, faith, humility and self-control.

Teaching is time consuming. There are papers to grade, reports to maintain, lessons to prepare, bulletin boards to create, and many other unending duties to do. It's easy to begin to leave out your devotion time--not purposely, but from what seems to be necessity. Be careful; your light will become dim. You must stay connected to the source of spiritual light to shine. We are only the conduits of light. Without the source of power, our light will fade into darkness. Satan will encourage you toward activities—even good ones—so you have no time to grow spiritually. A sense of duty can be a trap. To always be there for your coworkers, your boss, your family members, your students, your friends, and your fellowman but neglecting your personal time in the Scriptures and prayer is like trying to give them a glass of water with an empty pitcher. You have nothing to pour out to others until you are filled up with God.

Go back to the place where you lost your first love. It is still there; rekindle the fire. Find a quiet spot outdoors. Read Psalms 8 and Psalms 19 aloud. Read the Psalms aloud. Review the four Gospels. Begin to meditate on the Words of Jesus, the love of God, the beauty of His creation, and His faithfulness. As you wait before God privately, you will be renewed.

Dear God, Renew my mind and my spirit today. Help me to have once again that first love for you that made every morning new. As I wait before you and study your word, give me fresh manna for today.

80 OBEDIENCE BRINGS ILLUMINATION

Revelation 3:1-3 *. . .I know your deeds; you have a reputation of being alive, but you are dead. ² Wake up! Strengthen what remains and is about to die, for I have not found your deeds complete in the sight of my God. ³ Remember, therefore, what you have received and heard; obey it, and repent.*

A lightbulb has two posts with a filament stretched over both ends. As long as that filament stays intact, the bulb can produce light. But, if the filament breaks, the bulb cannot provide light even when connected to the power source. God's Word contains rules that serve as boundaries to protect those who follow Christ. The filament of the lightbulb represents our connection with God. Our obedience strengthens the connection, and we shine for Christ. But, when we disobey, we break the continuous flow of His power. We cannot shine for Jesus when we rebel. Our testimony, our inner joy and our peace are dulled because of disobedience.

If your disobedience or neglect has damaged your closeness with God, ask God to forgive you. He began the work of the Spirit in you, and He waits anxiously to renew your spiritual walk again. Call out His name, and He will come running to meet your needs.

Obedience brings growth and blessing. Disobedience brings darkness and confusion. Choose light. Repent for your acts of defiance and commit them to God. Invite God to light up your life again. It's worth the struggle.

Dear God, I know where I failed. I see my rebellion. Please forgive me. I am wrong. I want to turn from my disobedience and follow your ways. Renew your light in me so that I can find my way. I choose obedience today.

81 ARE WE TEACHING STUDENTS TO BE KIND?

Ephesians 4:32 *And be ye kind one to another, tenderhearted, forgiving one another, even as God for Christ's sake hath forgiven you. (Also Colossians 3:12-13).*

I remember the day I fully understood the grace of God. Even though I gave my life to God at an early age, I was in my mid-thirties before the true revelation of God's unconditional love and forgiveness became a reality to me. I hadn't done anything major wrong, and I wasn't running from God; instead, I just became aware of God's awesome, unconditional love that he had for people. I was awestruck! After that, I understood more about God's forgiveness and His desire for me to forgive others. We honor Christ when we are gracious to others.

Kindness is a decision. It does not depend upon the other person's behavior. We can be kind to people because God loves them. Kindness feels right inside. Hateful acts make me feel unhappy and out of sorts. We can choose kindness even when the other person is not kind. We only have control of our actions and not anyone else's actions.

Once you have learned the benefit and the art of kindness, you can teach it to your students. Students need to understand the concept of civility. Civility is civilized conduct that includes being polite, courteous, and respectful. An uncivilized society attacks, brutalizes, and destroys fellow citizens. As educators, we can be change agents in our society by helping students to understand the proper way people should treat one another. Practice kindness in your classroom. Teach your students to allow others to go first, to open the door for each other, to greet each other with a smile, and to say thank you to each other. You may be one of the few people in their lives that will expose them to true civility.

Dear God, Thank you for your unconditional love. Give me the wisdom and understanding how to train my students in acts of civility and kindness. I commit myself to be a change agent in my small world and introduce civility back into our everyday world.

82 DON'T FORGET THE LITTLE THINGS

Psalm 32:8 *I will instruct you and teach you in the way you should go; I will counsel you with my loving eye on you.*

As teachers, our responsibilities seem unending with lesson planning and preparation, classroom discipline, grading papers, completing reports, attending meetings, working with parents, serving on assigned committees, fulfilling special assigned duties, etc. No matter how demanding our schedule becomes, we must be determined to keep the main thing the main thing.

Teaching academics is important, but our influence reaches farther than just training academics. In every classroom, there are individual needs to be discovered. Some students require unique academic support that may need one-on-one attention. Other students may need emotional or social support. With God's help and our willingness to serve, we can be used to encourage and support those needs. As you become God's hand extended, you will leave lasting memories that can be used as examples for future generations.

I had several teachers who went the extra mile with me when I was a student. My eighth-grade math teacher realized that several students in my class had not mastered seventh-grade math. He invited all of us to meet with him at 7:00 every Tuesday and Thursday morning to help us catch up. We all worked together for three or four months. I often think of the sacrifice of his time and energy freely given to us. His gift to the other students and me encouraged me to "Pay it forward" to my students who needed extra support.

My eleventh-grade health teacher saw me crying in the hallway one day and stopped to help. My heart was broken. I had just come from the high school counselor's office where she discouraged me from becoming a teacher. My health teacher put her arms around me and told me that if I wanted to be a teacher, then I should go to college and become a teacher. She told me to follow my heart, and I did. Her words helped me to put aside the counselor's negative report and continue to pursue my dream. She gave up part of her lunch hour to comfort me and encourage me to follow my dreams.

There may be instances in your life when a teacher made a significant difference in your future. These are examples of the "little things" that can make a more significant impact on a student's life than any lesson you may teach in the classroom. Don't get too busy to see unique opportunities God brings for you to make a real difference in students' lives.

Dear God, I am grateful for my teachers who were more than just a teacher to me. Help me to see those golden opportunities and give me the courage and stamina to meet the challenges. I want to be your hand extended out to my students.

83 GIVE ME FRESH PERSPECTIVES

Deuteronomy 32:2 *Let my teaching fall like rain and my words descend like dew, like showers on new grass, like abundant rain on tender plants.*

Life (or death) will be delivered through our words as we interact with our students this year. James 3:10 warns us of our natural tendency to speak both blessing and cursing as we encounter frustrations and roadblocks throughout our day. We must commit ourselves to pour out life-giving hope and encouragement to our students, and refrain from discouraging comments like "You always. . ." or "You never. . ." or "Why can't you just. . ."

I recently heard the Christian comedian, Ken Davis, tell how his English teacher kept him after class because of misbehavior. He knew he had acted like the class clown and disrespected her and her class. He expected the worse. Instead, his teacher looked at him sternly and said, "You have a gift." He was shocked by her statement. She then began to tell him that God had given him a gift to make people laugh, but he was misusing it. As his "punishment," she required him to join the speech club where he excelled in humorous rhetoric. His teacher chose to bless him by directing his misused natural gift toward activities that helped him discover and develop his natural talent. She could have suspended him or punished him with mundane work. Instead, she chose to see beyond his foolishness to influence him toward God's design for his life. She brought fresh rain into his life.

We can pray for fresh perspectives as we walk through the daily challenges of this year. If we are willing, God can bring golden opportunities to bless and not curse our students. We can choose not to be personally offended by a student's behavior so that we can bring life into a tense situation.

Dear God, Help me to see my students the way you see them. Direct my words and attitudes to bring blessings to each of my students. Give me abundant grace and compassion for those students that make my job more difficult. Open my eyes and help me to see beyond their foolishness, so I can be your instrument to help direct them toward productivity and positive growth.

84 BE THE BEST TEACHER/EMPLOYEE YOU CAN BE

Colossians 3:23 *Whatever you do, work at it with all your heart, as working for the Lord, not for human masters.*

Work is an attribute of God. Creating and producing is a gift to humanity—not a curse. The very fabric of our nature as image bearers of God is to work. David wrote in Psalm 8:6 that God made us rulers over the works of our hands.

There are several things a teacher can do to become an employee that pleases God.

   (1) Do what you are asked to do. That is what you are paid to do. Do your work as unto the Lord.
   (2) Do your best to please your employers. Don't do just the minimum. Be willing to learn something new. (Joseph, in the Bible, continued to grow his skills in spite of being a slave.)

(3) Keep a positive attitude. Don't speak against your employer. Offer creative solutions when there is a problem rather than complaints.
(4) Be a trustworthy employee. Be dependable. Prove yourself by earning respect from your coworkers and your boss. Trustworthy people receive promotions.
(5) Work in such a way that Christ is glorified. Your job is a mission field, and you are the missionary. Let your light shine as you serve your school and your students.

Dear God, I want to honor you as I teach at my school. Things are not always fair in job assignments and expectations. Help me to keep my eyes on you and do my job well. I want to be all you want me to be.

85 CHOOSE NOT TO BE OFFENDED

James 1:19-20 ...Everyone should be quick to listen, slow to speak and slow to become angry because human anger does not produce the righteousness that God desires.

It takes practice to learn to be slow to anger. Anger comes often without warning, but what you do with that anger determines whether you win or lose. You can choose to allow the offense to penetrate your heart, or you can discard it and not let it dwell in your thoughts.

"That was not kind!" I said to myself. I could feel the offense rising in my heart. "Why would he say that? What did I do to deserve that kind of response?" I went on about my daily tasks, but my heart was still grappling with my emotions. "I need to be more mature than to allow an offense to build between my coworker and me," I told myself. "Besides, he was probably having a bad day, and it was a small thing." But my heart kept feeling the offense. My emotional struggle with the offense continued for over an hour.

Finally, I made a conscious decision to let it go. "I choose not to be offended. I would not wait for my coworker to apologize to me before I let my anger go. I chose not to let the dagger of offense penetrate my heart and destroy our relationship!" My mind was working through the offense step by step. I realized that this coworker had said thoughtless, but innocent, things in the past. I chose to trust his heart, not his words. The process of working through my anger and choosing to forgive him set the offense out of my heart. The next day all was well as if it had never happened.

Without God's grace, I would not have had the strength to process through such an offense. But, with God, we can release offense because we have been released by the blood of Christ. We can choose not to be offended. If the wound is too deep to just let it go, Matthew 18 tells us to go to the one who offended us and work it out. We must be willing to choose to work through it and not let a wedge come between us and those on our team. As much as it depends on you, live at peace with all men.

Dear God, Give me the wisdom and the willingness to walk through the process of releasing offense. I need the grace to face times of stress and conflict

86 ALL STUDENTS CAN LEARN TO BE COURTEOUS

Psalms 19:8-9 *The precepts of the LORD are right, giving joy to the heart. The commands of the LORD are radiant, giving light to the eyes. ⁹ The fear of the LORD is pure, enduring forever. The ordinances of the LORD are sure and altogether righteous.*

All students can follow a standard of conduct. It doesn't matter if your school is public or private, Christian or an evangelistic outreach ministry with non-Christian students, a positive atmosphere is possible. It wasn't too many years ago, that courtesy was the norm, but civility seems to be quickly fading. Anyone can follow the basic guidelines of common courtesy and good manners through training. The statutes of the Lord are right in any setting.

Schools must expect students to become self-disciplined. School leaders need to believe that students do not have to be a Christian to clean up their mouths while at school. Anyone can choose to speak decently; they can choose to stop the off-colored jokes. An unbeliever can refrain from alcohol, drugs, sex, or cigarettes. Any student can choose not to fight or stir up strife. It is possible for any student to build self-control. Your school can have a pleasant, well-behaved school even with non-Christians in attendance by requiring a certain standard of behavior and lifestyle.

Parents and students need to consider the benefit of building a safe, pleasant school climate. Teachers and administrators can make an appeal to get their cooperation in striving for a better school. I suggest that each student and parent be required to sign a contract that gives the details of the code of conduct listing the consequences for failing to comply. For private or charter schools, any student desiring to attend the school should understand the policies of the school before entering, decide whether or not he is willing to abide by those standards, and then sign a written agreement. If a student breaks the conduct code, he should receive the consequences predetermined by the written guidelines. (Students will watch to see if you follow the written guidelines. If you don't, you wasted your time writing it.)

Although these are administrative decisions, I have included this concept to help teachers be an influence in making their school a better place for those seeking a positive school atmosphere. You can use these guidelines in an appeal to your administrator by requesting the board consider changing school policies regarding standards of conduct. A positive school climate is imperative for a thriving learning environment. Common courtesy and kindness can change your school's atmosphere. Working together as an entire team and an entire school system can bring positive changes in the culture and the student's lives at your school.

Dear God, Help me to be an instrument in my school as I work to bring a positive attitude and climate to my students. Show us specific directions my school can take to help build common courtesy and kindness in our students and staff.

87 MY EVALUATION DID NOT GO AS EXPECTED

Hebrews 13:17 *Have confidence in your leaders and submit to their authority, because they keep watch over you as those who must give an account. Do this so that their work will be a joy, not a burden, for that would be of no benefit to you.*

You thought you did a great job during your evaluation, but your supervisor marked you down in a few areas. First of all, I know you are disappointed. No one likes to receive anything less than a good evaluation. You may even feel that the report was judgmental and inaccurate. The question now is, "What can you do about it?"

The scripture above reminds us that God puts leaders in place. That means that your supervisor has some things to teach you, and, God may use you to enlighten your supervisor. Any form of disrespect or attack you display toward your supervisor will negate any appeal or clarification you may offer to gain more credibility. Even discussing your frustration with other coworkers can work against you if word gets back to your supervisor that you are bad mouthing him or his opinion. Below are some suggestions you might consider.

1. During your review, listen carefully to your supervisor's explanations. Don't argue. Respectfully ask for clarification if you don't understand something. Take notes. Include the positive statements in your notes as well as the negative. Ask for suggestions on how you could improve for a better review next time. Stay friendly and speak softly. If it is not offered, ask

for a copy of the review. Thank your supervisor for meeting with you.
2. After leaving the meeting, get somewhere you can be alone for a few minutes for prayer. Submit yourself to God and acknowledge that your supervisor is there to help you be the best you can be. Choose to submit to your leader's authority as an act of worship to God. Ask God for the grace and wisdom to learn from the review. As for clarity and insight on how you can improve and how best you can meet your supervisor's expectation in the future. If you feel there is a personality conflict with your leader, ask God for grace to mend the fences that may have crumbled during the year.
3. If possible, meet with someone you trust (preferably not part of the school) and discuss the review. Begin with all of the positive statements. It is important to remind yourself that there were positive things said. Next, take each lower score and decide if you feel you might need to work on those areas. Begin to make a plan for improvement. Choose to learn from the review.
4. When I did evaluations, I learned that an outside observer could see much more in the classroom than teachers can see. They also can misunderstand what happens if they have not been at the school in the past. Accept the accurate parts of the report, own it, and decide to do better. However, if there is a particular part that you feel was misunderstood entirely, you may want to make an appointment to appeal. (See Devotion #14). An appeal is not a demand; it is a request for consideration. You must approach your authority with the willingness to be told "no."
5. After you have done all you can do, get "back in the saddle." Do your lesson plans, smile at your students, and get busy teaching. God is in control, and He will watch over you.

Dear God, Help me to act correctly regarding the review I just received. I want to purposely act with respect rather than react with bitterness or resentment. I submit my heart to you. Give me the grace to get past this experience.

88 GOD HELP ME TO HONOR STUDENTS WHO STRUGGLE

I Corinthians 12:21-22 The eye cannot say to the hand, "I don't need you!" And the head cannot say to the feet, "I don't need you!" [22] On the contrary, those parts of the body that seem to be weaker are indispensable.

Without realizing it, teachers often dishonor students who struggle academically or behaviorally. Johnny can't read as well as the rest of the class, Sarah can't stay focused on written work, and William shows his temper when he is irritated or makes a mistake. Each of these hypothetical students has unique needs that require individual consideration from the teacher. The challenge is how to meet each of the needs without dishonoring the student.

There are no magical answers; however, there is a general principle I would like to share. When possible, promote the student's strengths and protect his weaknesses from public display. Some examples follow.

Johnny has trouble reading, but he is required to participate in a reading circle just like the other students. One way to honor him is to give him a heads-up for which passage he will be asked to read so he can preview it before the circle meets. During oral reading times, give Johnny only passages that he has had an opportunity to rehearse. This helps him to "save face" with his peers while he is remediating in reading. If he proves good at discussing history or science, allow him to excel in classroom discussions. Allow the class to see his strengths.

Sarah can't stay focused on her work. Instead of calling out her name and asking her to get busy, meet with her and agree upon a "signal" that lets her know you are calling her back to her work without calling her name. One such signal is to touch the edge of her desk or chair as you walk past her. Calling out her name, again and again, brings negative peer attention to her deficit.

William has a temper. Meet with him privately to plan how he can best handle irritations and disappointments. Allow him to get a drink when he is frustrated. This may help him to walk off the adrenalin and cool down before returning to class. Set boundaries for him such as no verbal sighs or mumbling, and no slamming papers or physical jesters when he gets angry. If he stays within those boundaries, you can give him a reprieve, when possible.

Students care about what students and teachers think about them. The more you honor your struggling students by showing concern for them socially as well as academically, the more likely these students will join your team.

Dear God, Help me to understand which of my students need extra honor and care. Give me the wisdom and energy to avoid embarrassing any of my students. I choose to honor EVERY student you have given to me this year.

89 GOD, I HAVE A DECISION TO MAKE

James 1:5 If any of you lacks wisdom, you should ask God, who gives generously to all without finding fault, and it will be given to you.

Are you frustrated? Are you having trouble determining God's will in the decision? My husband and I faced a similar crisis about two years into our marriage. I fretted and prayed, then prayed and fretted more. Either decision posed serious consequences to our future. My husband sat down with me and said, "Elderine, this is what we are going to do. We are going to ask God to lead our thoughts toward His will. We are going to trust Him to do that. Then we are going to discuss the options together and make the decision that seems right to us. Then we are going to trust that God led us to come to that decision." And, that is what we did; later it was clear that we made the best decision.

Choose to believe and trust God's guidance as you ask Him to direct your thoughts toward His will. It sounds simple, but it has been a guiding principle of our lives throughout our many years of marriage. However, one thing you need to realize, it was our thoughts and not our feelings that guided us. Feelings can be deceiving and toss us about from one emotion to another. Do your best to move from your feelings to your "thinking." As you consider the choices and the possible outcomes, pray over each one. Discuss the decision with someone you trust, if possible. You may want to sleep after your brainstorming session to let things settle in your mind. When you think you have found the right decision, then check your feelings. If there is still no peace, continue seeking wisdom until both your thoughts and your emotions are at peace with the decision.

Proverbs 3:5-6 says, *Trust in the Lord with all your heart and lean not on your own understanding; in all your ways submit to him, and he will make your paths straight.* God will not give you a stone if you ask him for bread. He is faithful.

Dear God, I choose to trust you to guide me in this decision. I ask for supernatural guidance and wisdom as I think about my options and the possible consequences of each one. I know you are faithful. I trust you.

90 HELP ME LEARN FROM MY EXPERIENCES

Isaiah 40:31 But they that wait upon the LORD shall renew their strength; they shall mount up with wings as eagles; they shall run, and not be weary; and they shall walk, and not faint.

The year is almost over. Battles and victories have been etched into your mental scrapbook of teaching experiences. Have you praised God for those experiences--both the struggles and the victories? Did you gain valuable wisdom and insight through each one of them? If not, perhaps you might want to make a list of the experiences and review them in your quiet time this summer. God can give you understanding, insight, and instructions as you wait before Him. The Holy Spirit can use all of these experiences as stepping stones to an even better year next year. Be honest with God and with yourself. Allow the scriptures to be profitable for you as you receive doctrine, reproof, correction and instruction from God through your daily Bible reading (2 Timothy 3:16).

Do not allow yourself to become weary in well doing. Many become exhausted toward the end of the school year-- administrators, staff, teachers, students, and parents. Exhaustion can lead to quick tempers, thoughtless words and actions, and unkind, harsh responses to those you serve. Guard your heart and reputation with diligence. In times like these, become determined to listen a lot and speak only after you have given thought to your words (James 1:19). Eat balanced meals, get plenty of rest, and pace yourself during this last stretch. Make lists of things to be done. Take that list into your prayer chamber and ask God to guide you through the task of accomplishing each requirement. You are invited to cast your care upon Him--Because He cares for you (I Peter 5:7).

The wonderful thing about God is that He gives a new beginning each day. As you prepare your final lesson plans and end of year activities, don't forget to wait upon the Lord to renew your strength. If you will, you can mount up with wings as eagles. You can run and not be weary. You can walk and not faint (Isaiah 40:31). Spiritual renewal is the key to finishing the race well.

Dear God, You are my hiding place. Teach me, Lord, to wait before you, to search your Word for instruction and guidance, and to rest in you as I walk the final mile of this year's teaching assignment.

DEVOTIONS FOR HOLIDAYS AND SPECIAL EVENTS

91 HOLIDAYS CAN CREATE STRESS

Ephesians 5:29: *Do not let any unwholesome talk come out of your mouths, but only what is helpful for building others up according to their needs, that it may benefit those who listen.*

Teachers and students eagerly anticipate holidays and spring and summer breaks. For teachers, it is often a time for tight schedules, finishing up a term, planning and purchasing gifts, and sometimes getting ready for out of town guests. Stress can become more prominent in our lives than the joy of the school holiday. Stress can cause us to say things we later wished we hadn't said. Being rushed and pressured with deadlines can bring out the worst in anyone. Teachers are no exception.

We cannot afford the luxury of breaking down the invaluable "blocks" of communication and relationships we have worked so hard to build throughout the semester. To avoid conflict during this time, take time to list the things you have to do in three categories—PRIORITY (Must do now), NEED TO DO (Get done by this date), and NICE TO DO (Would really like to do this). Take each item and place a date beside it indicating when you should have it accomplished. Make your plan (be reasonable); then work the plan. Be sure to include any parties, meetings or obligations you may have. Decide if some of the "Nice to do" things can be postponed until the stress of the break comes to an end. Be realistic and avoid perfectionism.

Having the plan will help you to know, in reality, how far behind" or how "caught up" you are. You may even be able to get ahead of your schedule and enjoy the feeling of accomplishment. We often stress over things that seem bigger than they really are. Teachers know about planning. You understand the need to establish a short-term plan and a longer term plan. Use those skills to help you through deadlines that school breaks require.

Commit to speaking words of life even when you are under stress. Speak them to your coworkers, your students, your family and your friends. Speak words that will benefit those who hear them. Bless and don't curse. As you do, you will experience the joy of each season.

Dear God, Give me the wisdom and the grace to handle the pressures of the next few weeks. Enable me to speak kind and caring words to those I serve. Help me to establish a workable plan. Multiply my time to enable me to accomplish those many things required during this month. Thank you for supporting me through this time of year.

92 TIME TO REJOICE AND REFLECT ON GOOD THINGS

Philippians 4:4-7 *Rejoice in the Lord always. I will say it again: Rejoice! [5]Let your gentleness be evident to all. The Lord is near. [6]Do not be anxious about anything, but in every situation, by prayer and petition, with thanksgiving, present your requests to God. [7]And the peace of God, which transcends all understanding, will guard your hearts and your minds in Christ Jesus.*

For many, the past few months have presented trials and pain. Heavy hearts and daily struggles may make this holiday season challenging to face. My prayers are with families who have been without work, have experienced extreme illness, or have lost a loved one and are facing their first Thanksgiving or Christmas without them.

Apostle Paul understood trials and pain. He wrote that he had learned to be content in his current situation. He writes the above verses to teach us how to deal with difficult times.

- His first instruction is to Rejoice in the Lord! No matter how difficult our circumstances, it is a blessing to have the Lord with us at all times. We can choose to rejoice in God's ever-present help in our time of need.
- Secondly, be gentle even in your struggles. Let the gentleness of Christ flow through you as you deal with others who may not understand your current sufferings
- Thirdly, don't be anxious--do not fret! Instead of worrying about what might happen or what has happened, pray about everything. Lay your fears, your failures, and your future at God's feet.
- Fourth, begin to breathe prayers of thanksgiving (counting your blessings) throughout the day. You can even thank God for the little things--sunlight, water, electricity, etc. It is incredible how much we take for granted. If you have lost a loved one, remember the good times and thank God for every day you shared with them. Thank God for each day, month or year you were given.

Concentrate on your blessings and not your losses. Choose to change your thoughts much like you would change your television to another channel. Just click the button and begin to occupy your mind with Thanksgiving. Speak it out loud. Sing songs of praise and adoration to God; put on CDs that express thanksgiving to God. Open your shades and let the sunshine come into your home.

Paul continues with these words- Philippians 4:8-9 *Finally, brothers and sisters, whatever is true, whatever is noble, whatever is right, whatever is pure, whatever is lovely, whatever is admirable—if anything is excellent or praiseworthy—think about such things. 9 Whatever you have learned or received or heard from me, or seen in me—put it into practice. And the God of peace will be with you.*

Paul tells us in verses seven and nine what we will gain if we are willing to take our thoughts captive and turn them to thanksgiving and praise. Our reward is "Peace that transcends all understanding." The peace of God will guard your heart and your mind and carry you through this holiday season. God is faithful to do what His Word promises if we are willing to follow His instructions. Ask God for the strength to be thankful for the little things. You will find peace even in your memories if you cover them with thankfulness.

Dear God, Thank you for your faithfulness. Thank you for your guidance that points us toward victory over the troublesome trials in our lives. Give us the courage to choose peace over fretting. Help us to be sensitive to the needs of others during this holiday season. Give us wisdom on how we may comfort those who are hurting during this holiday season.

BONUS DEVOTIONS

Note: The following devotions may be more applicable to teachers in Christian schools where there is more flexibility in student selection. However, all teachers may gain insight from them. Enjoy!

93 DRIVE OUT THE SCORNER OR SAVE HIM?

Prov 22:10 "Drive out the mocker, and out goes strife; quarrels and insults are ended."

Scorners and mockers cause turmoil and unrest in a school. The longer they remain in a school, the more they influence others to become mockers, and the more the leaders will feel overwhelmed with disobedience and lawlessness.

Mockers will become increasingly common during the "end times" according to Jude 18. Jude describes these lawless "men" as people who creep in unawares. It may not be obvious that they are mockers at first. Then we discern that they are "ungodly, turning the grace of our Lord God into lasciviousness (sexual lust and desire) and denying God (no fear of God or His ways or [authority])." Jude reminds us that God cast out angels who turned against Him; prophets destroyed rebellious nations. God destroyed Sodom and Gomorrah because of their mockery and sin against Him. God expects us to deal with those who bring discord into our school.

How do we recognize them? Jude 1:8 says these "filthy dreamers"
1. Defile the flesh (live unclean lives).
2. Despise dominion (hates to be told what to do—mocks authority).
3. Speaks evil of dignities (things set apart by God—even truth from Scriptures).
4. They have gone the way of Cain; they run greedily after error.

Jude describes these students as spots in your "feast"; "clouds without rain"; "... trees, without fruit...--twice dead;" "... wild waves of the sea, foaming up their shame"; and "wandering stars, for whom the blackest darkness has been reserved forever.... These men are grumblers and faultfinders; they follow their own evil desires; they boast about themselves and flatter others for their own advantage. (Jude 1:12-16)

Jude 1: 22 and 23 give written instructions for dealing with these students. We are to have compassion on some by training them. Others find their salvation when leaders use strong boundaries and tough love to pull them from their destructive path. Unfortunately, a third group must be "driven out" so that quarrels and dissension will cease. It will take discernment and the leading of God's Spirit to deal with these students correctly.

The following discipline guideline seems to be scripturally appropriate in light of Jude:
1. Warn them once by training them and showing them the Scriptures regarding mockery.
2. Watch for change. If no change, discipline them strongly.
3. Place them on probation and let them know the required changes needed to remain in the school.
4. If no change, dismiss them. If you dismiss them, there will be peace again.

Dear God, Open our eyes and let us see your ways. Help us to understand how your Word applies to our school situation. Let us not be quick to "rid" ourselves of the troublemaker, but let our hearts desire to "restore," "correct" and "preserve" those we can, but give us the courage to "send out" those that are leading others astray. (See note.)

Note to reader: I realize this is an intense devotion. Many educators have not studied the affect scorners and mockers have on a school. An excellent resource for this topic is Rick Horne's book, *Scorners and Mockers: How to dampen their influence in your school.*

94 GIVE US WISDOM WHEN SELECTING STUDENTS

Proverbs 18:3 *When wickedness comes, so does contempt, and with shame comes disgrace.*

Solomon knew the danger of wicked companions. He realized the "simple" (undeveloped and unprepared) ones would be led astray by the wicked influences. We must protect our student body from those who choose to be a negative leader.

In my early years of teaching, I struggled the idea of students being expelled or denied admission. It seemed heartless and not like Christ to reject students who apparently needed the gospel. As my experience broadened, I began to see the devastation that one student can have on a complete student body. I learned that student selection is one of the most important jobs of an administrator. I now believe that we must not sacrifice the whole for one. I feel that evangelism is done best by the churches and other evangelistic settings. The Christian school setting, even though evangelistic, should concentrate on discipleship and character training. A student, who has not chosen to turn toward truth, will not accept instruction in it.

When new students enter your school, watch for attitude changes within the student body. If you see unrest, discontent, anger, resentment or bitterness growing, begin to check for negative influences. You may be dealing with a "wicked root" or at least a student or group of students that need an attitude adjustment. We must deal with the rebellion and bad attitudes that surface because when there is contempt and unrest in a student body, education is stifled.

If a "wicked" influence thrives in your school, speak to your administrator about working to control the negative influence. Work together on a plan to adjust attitudes through "tough love" measures. When attitudes subside, you will notice a difference in the overall atmosphere. This peaceful atmosphere is worth the effort. However, if all efforts for change have failed, it is better to dismiss the one to save the whole from his harmful influence.

Dear God, Let us know the truth. Let us teach salvation to those who are willing and release those who are not. Give us the courage and wisdom to see the difference, and let it all be done in love.

95 CHILDREN ARE OUR MISSION FIELD

Psalm 25:4-6 *One generation will commend your works to another, they will tell of your mighty acts. They will speak of the glorious splendor of your majesty. .They will tell of the power of your awesome works and I will proclaim your great deeds.*

Your greatest mission field is the children, teens and young adults you have in your life. As parents, aunts/uncles, teachers, or friends of children, you have a story to share that can leave a lasting impression. When God gives you the opportunity, share your personal story with them. Don't preach to them--SHARE.

Share the testimony of your salvation. Discuss those nuggets of truth that God dropped in your heart throughout your life experiences. Tell of your victories and miracles. Tell them stories about your ancestors and God's faithfulness to them. Don't forget to tell about your hardships and how you overcame them. Don't forget to share your love and your time. Tell funny stories; play with them and laugh with them. Also, give them a glimpse of your dreams for their future. These are things the children will never forget. Make time to SHARE.

This is scriptural. Deuteronomy 11:19 (KJV) says *And ye shall teach them your children, speaking of them when thou sittest in thine house, and when thou walkest by the way, when thou liest down.*

Ask God to let you see students the way He sees them. It will melt your heart. Guard your words carefully when you speak to or about them. Children have no filter. They believe what they are told. Tell them you see them growing up to be a good person. Let them know you can see goodness in them—even when it may be hidden at the time. Praise them for the least bit of gentleness and kindness they show in their lives. Speak love, acceptance, and forgiveness to them. Don't magnify their weaknesses; it will become a huge stumbling block for them. Point out gifts and talents you see in them.

Love them and accept them even when they stray, embarrass you, and seemingly reject all that you love. Remind yourself that Jesus said he would leave the ninety-nine and find the one that strayed. Pray for God to find and restore those that wander during their difficult times. They need your love the most when they wander.

Dear God, I want to be your hand extended to the children you have put in my life this year. Melt my heart to see how much you care about each one—even the most difficult students.

SUBJECT INDEX

Acceptance, 5, 51, 141

Anger, 1, 4, 33, 36, 44, 53, 58, 79, 100, 103, 107, 124, 140

Angry, 57, 63, 94

Anxious, 66

Appreciation, 81

Attitude, 34, 65, 72, 83, 96, 115

Authority, 21, 25, 30, 56, 67, 76, 106, 127, 128

Balance, 73

Bitterness, 23

Blame, 84, 115

Blessing, 24, 122

BOSS, 21

Boundaries, 4, 50, 94, 118, 129

Bully, 85, 98

Cause and effect, viii, 78, 90

Character, 24, 55, 103

Civility, 120

Comfort, 70

Communication, 10, 32, 71, 72, 85, 97, 133

Compassion, 82, 88, 104, 106, 108

Complaint, 99

Conflict, vi, 16, 39, 85, 87, 103, 107, 133

Confrontation, 99

Consequences, 78, 90, 94

Consistency, 90, 95

Contentment, 13, 67, 71

Corporal punishment, 51

Courage, 53, 59

Coworker, 11, 34, 54, 79, 102, 117, 123, 124, 127, 134

Decision, 130

Differentiated instruction, 89

Discipline, 6, 16, 20, 24, 29, 32, 42, 50, 51, 52, 90, 91, 94, 98, 109, 122, 140
Mocker, 139

Division, 32

Elijah, 70

Employee, 123

End of year, 111, 132

Evaluation, 127

Exhaustion, 132

Extra mile, 20, 73, 102, 111, 121

Failure, 89

Favoritism, 62

Flexibility, 19

Foolishness, 15, 62

Forgive, 56, 85, 102, 115, 116

Forgiveness, 57

God's timing, 112

God's Word, 96

Grace, 3, 23, 61

Polishing the Apple 2

Grades, 16, 74, 104

Gratitude, *81*

Guidance, *109*

Heart issues, 23, *32*, *34*, *48*, *59*, *63*, *64*, *72*, *86*, *89*, 105, *110*, *114*, *116*

Holidays, *133*

Homework., *18*

Honor, *129*

Hope, *53*, *82*, *83*, *87*, *122*

Humility, *74*, *80*, *87*, *106*

Influence, *121*

Justice, 74

Kindness, *81*, *106*, *111*, *119*, *126*

King Saul, *116*

Leader, *21*

Leaders, *31*, *105*, *126*

Learning difficulties, *129*

Love, 6, *11*, *23*, *28*, *37*, *57*, 62, *83*, *119*

Mephibosheth, *116*

Mercy, 33, 56, 61, 74, *102*

Mocker, *44*, *85*, *138*
  Scorner, *139*

Natural consequences, *113*

Notes, *60*

Obedience, 27, *30*, 48, 55, 64, *76*, 114, *118*

Obey, 36, *44*, 49, 55, 56, 64, 65, *76*, *87*, 114

Offense, 16, 34, 57, 58, *79*, 84, 85, 94, 98, 100, 124, 125

Parent conference, *99*

Parents, *54*

Passive rebellion, 26

Pay it forward, 121

Perspective, *122*

Planning., *134*

Positive attitude, *123*

Potential, *110*

Prayer, 47, *54*, *78*, *97*, *106*, *117*

Rebellion, *22*, *26*, 48, 51, 52, 76

Resentment, *22*

Respect, *30*, *50*, *80*, *120*

Responsibility, *73*, *95*

Rest, 3

Restoration, 113

Restore, 32, 35, 57, 67, 116, 139

Rules, *4*, *76*, *90*, *94*

Samson, *68*

School climate, *20*, *125*

Seeds, *31*, *108*, *111*

Self-acceptance, *24*

Self-control, *68*, *91*, *106*, *126*

Self-discipline, *17*, *51*, *126*

Self-pity, *84*, *115*

Sense of duty, *72*, 117

Sense of humor, 11, 16

Share, *141*

Soft answer, 84

Solomon, *38*, *50*, *109*, *139*

Stress, *133*

Success, *89*

Team, *81*

Thankful, *66, 81*

Tongue, 23, 33, *71, 105, 107*

Trust, *66,* 78, *112, 130*

U*nforgiveness*, 5

Unity, *1*

Victim, *52*

Willing, 6, 13, 20, 22, 25, 29, 45, 48, 52, 57, 59, *64, 114*

Wisdom, 8, 9, 20, 22, 30, 39, 43, 47, 56, 60, *86, 109*, 136, 137

W*ise*, vi

Words, *33, 71*, 122

Work, *123*

Made in the USA
Las Vegas, NV
14 September 2021